RECLAIMING CHRISTMAS

How to Creatively Celebrate the Season That Has Become Excessmas

GINGER JURRIES

ILLUSTRATOR
ROBERT ASHLEY

WestBow
PRESS
A DIVISION OF THOMAS NELSON

WestBow Press books may be ordered through booksellers or by contacting:

WestBow Press
A Division of Thomas Nelson
1663 Liberty Drive
Bloomington, IN 47403
www.westbowpress.com
1 (866) 928-1240

ISBN: 978-1-4908-1441-4 (sc)
ISBN: 978-1-4908-1440-7 (hc)
ISBN: 978-1-4908-1442-1 (e)

Library of Congress Control Number: 2013920409

Printed in the United States of America.

WestBow Press rev. date: 12/02/2013

DEDICATION

I dedicate this book to all who desire a
more Christ-centered Christmas season and
to all those wise men and women who still seek Him.

Acknowledgements

I am deeply grateful to my friends who have contributed to the success of this book with their editorial expertise: Kristin Allen, Jim Jurries, Karen Mulder, Helen Komejan, Lisa Marie Eisenhower, Cynthia Heald and Gregg Nieusma.

CONTENTS

INTRODUCTION

How to Use this book

The book you are holding is a handbook for enhancing your family activities during the season of Advent. It is appropriate for a large age span and as such you might want to peruse the contents in order to determine which activities are appropriate for your children or grandchildren.

The section, *A Guide to Handling Holiday Grief,* Chapter 6, or *The Jewish-Christian Marriage Dilemma* in Chapter 7, What to say/What to Do, might not pertain to you so you could skip either chapter. On the other hand, the story about Hanukkah in the same chapter is quite fascinating and appropriate for anyone interested in the history of Christianity.

Memories of repeatable events and acts of kindness can be recorded in the *Remembering Advent – A Holiday Events Diary,* Chapter 10. Reviewing them encourages everyone to be more thoughtful throughout the year. Reminiscences about where and how the day was spent might also be recorded in this section. Activities that were a big success as well as those too difficult or inappropriate for the children could be noted.

Resources That Make Memories, Chapter 11, contains a rich resource for treasured family reading. Although the list of Christmas books is inexhaustible, those listed are some of my favorites. You might begin a tradition of buying a book for the entire family (or for yourself) at the beginning of each Advent season. My daughter, Kristin, and I still chuckle about the Christmas that we gave each other the same book, *Where Angels Walk,* by Joan Wester Anderson!

Hopefully, the ideas in this book will guide you to *design* your holiday activities rather than simply allowing the commercialism of the season to mold you into its pattern of activities.

Why Change Our Celebrations?

"We've always done it that way," is a familiar saying that has been used over the centuries as an excuse to remain steadfast in our habits and traditions. There are some things that should remain as entrenched as a mole in his tunnel but other traditions, from time to time, cry for reexamination.

Perhaps you have, since you were young, followed certain Christmas traditions because you were raised to religiously carry them out year after year. You've never considered *not* doing them. They may or may not enhance your family's enjoyment of the season, your ability to get the most satisfaction from the holy season with a minimum of stress and hassle.

I believe that most families of faith have real concerns about the commercialism that has come to dominate the Christmas season. We have been blindly wooed by the glitter and gift-giving demands that have become woven tightly into our festivities. We feel compelled to keep pace with these customs because "it is expected of us." By whom, I wonder? What would happen if we reassessed our Christmas celebrations and put down our collective feet, refusing to ride the tidal wave of materialistic surfing? Would we be accused of being the Grinch who stole Christmas? I think not!

I invite you to take a hard look at the season we call holy and do an honest appraisal of your personal and family traditions. You just might find some ways to make changes in the way you invest your talents, your time and your money during the Christmas season. Perhaps you will find some good reasons to make some significant changes, ones that will be more satisfying, memorable, family centered and most importantly, more honoring to the Savior whose birth we commemorate.

CHAPTER 1

A LOOK OVER OUR COLLECTIVE SHOULDERS

Has your "Ho! Ho! Ho!" turned to "Oh! Oh! Oh!"? Christmas is supposed to be a delightful time of warm family gatherings and delightful memory-making activities. If, however, you're like most of the world's population, you feel like a freight train is barreling down on you when the calendar turns to December. With too much to do on top of the normal activities, the wants outweigh the bank account, and the parties and shopping tax the stamina of even the young and dauntless. The stress has made the holiday more of a month-long headache than a joyous event.

Strange Way to Celebrate

Ken Potts, writer for the Detroit Daily Herald, has this to say about the most stressful season: "If we are readying ourselves for a celebration of the birth of a man of peace – a person to whom many of us turn to for purpose, meaning, and the faith which is at the center of our lives; if we see this as a time to reaffirm and strengthen our ties and commitments to friends and family, it looks to me like we are going about this in a rather strange way."[1]

Will the Reason-for-the-Season Please Step forward?

Where is the Child?

I once read a story about a wealthy family who decided to have a party to celebrate their child's baptism. The guests arrived and the maid deposited the elegant wraps on the bed in the master bedroom. As the party progressed, one guest inquired as to the whereabouts of the baby. A frantic search ensued. No one could locate the child until someone remarked that she had seen him earlier on the bed in the master bedroom. And sure enough, there under a pile of coats and jackets was the baby, nearly smothered. The object of the party's celebration had been neglected and forgotten.

As I see shoppers bustling through crowded malls and hear complaints about how stressed my friends are and how there is no time for devotions and meaningful activities in the face of the long to-do list, I am reminded of this story.

The wise men came to Jerusalem with a singleness of purpose – to find the Christ child and worship Him. Likewise, it seems to me that our goal during the Christmas season needs to center on discovering anew the Christ in Christmas and in finding ways to duly honor and worship a Savior and King who is worthy of such honor.

Perhaps the cover of this book could be your focal point during the Christmas season. Whenever your focus tends to drift from centering on the spiritual aspects of the Christmas Season, let the example of the single-purposed wise men be your guide and inspiration to concentrate on finding the Christ of Christmas and making that your aim. Let your heart and the ideas in this book lead you to Him.

Christmas Quandary

Christmas doesn't have to be a countdown to exhaustion. Believe it or not, it could quite possibly be a peaceful season during which the family becomes more united and gains a new appreciation for the amazing significance of what, for Christians, should be one of the most holy (not crazy) and delightful seasons of the year. Sound impossible? Read on.

I suspect that most families with a sincere faith have longed not only to unplug the Christmas machine but also to establish family traditions and infuse more meaningful activities into the holidays. We, however, not only lack the direction we need but a "voice" that acknowledges that it's ok to change certain activities and replace them with those that enhance our worship of the Christ. In an age of materialism we have been sucked into the big commercial vacuum labeled EXCESSMAS. We have hardly noticed that we have abandoned our more spiritually rich customs and adopted worldly, materialistic ones. Alas, what a quandary.

When God became a Man

Christmas has become an event that is not only overly stressful and commercial but also that is almost too huge to define. For those of us who know the Christ, it is about remembering the time when God, through Christ, made Himself known to us by becoming a mere mortal. As Christians, we refer to this event as the incarnation, or emptying. It refers to someone who is brought low voluntarily, laying aside his high rank and becoming as nothing in comparison with his prior dignity. Coming to earth as the King of the Universe was an incredibly humiliating and degrading experience for Jesus. He was willing to endure not only it, but also the indignity of the cross, for our sakes. It seems appropriate to say that Christmas was when God become a man. Perhaps this is an oversimplification.

It is hard to understand what actually happened at that defining moment in time when God entered the universe as a man. We cannot understand the reality of the incarnation by looking at a nativity scene. The concept is way too complex for that small glimpse into time. What we need to do is try to understand the impact of Christ's coming to earth by finding out what He was up to before he was born. Jesus actually existed formerly as God, second person of the trinity. He did not suddenly appear on earth as Jesus. He transformed himself into a human who was not only fully human but fully God! What a concept! It was the only way that He could show Himself to us in a form that we could understand and with which we could identify and still be able to atone for our sins as a perfectly sinless person.

The Messiah became a being of another kind who took on a new nature – a human one – without changing who He was. Jesus, whom angels worship, left behind His infinitely glorious state by choice and humbled Himself on our behalf. That is how much He loves us.

Change Perspective for Heaven's Sake

As we will see in Chapter 8, Gift-Giving Revisited, it is actually not just the practice of gift-giving that robs Christmas of joyousness, but the frenzy of shopping for a gift, any gift, preferably one more extravagant than last year's.

Preparing for Christmas doesn't have to be a Martha Stewart marathon to Christmas excellence. There is a better way! The following is a path to a new holiday strategy, one that is not only more sane but that is honoring to the God who descended to earth in the form of a human to become our example for living and to become the bridge to the Father, taking our sins upon Himself.

Between the covers of this book you will find creative, nurturing activities to make your Christmas not just a season to endure until the tree gratefully comes down, but one to be cherished warmly all throughout the year. The ideas allow you to take a close look at past traditions and scrutinize them in the light of the first awesome Christmas.

Take a moment to evaluate your current Christmas traditions. Following is a sample list of present traditions to which many people religiously adhere. The second column is a list of possible modifications. You may want to peruse the list and consider alternatives to those things you once felt were an essential part of your celebration. How one may carry out these alternatives will be discussed in other sections of this book.

So there you have it. Christmas as we know it is up for grabs. It is yours to remake. What's important to you? What traditions do you want to leave with your children and grandchildren? What celebrations would best honor the One who gave us the most precious gift of all time? Which customs could you initiate that would redeem our sacred holiday?

CHAPTER 2

QUITTING COLD (OR WARM) TURKEY

We've always done it that Way

A Christmas Makeover/Activity Check List

It's no simple task, redesigning your holiday celebrations. So where do we begin? It seems to me that a good place to start is with the concept of Advent, which is the traditional season of the Christian holiday beginning in the first week in December. It is the time that we commemorate the season during which Jesus changed history forever by making His entrance to the earth in order to redeem mankind.

The following is a checklist of ways your family might possibly have celebrated the season in the past and invites you to consider some alternatives:

Present Traditions   Possible Modifications

Do everything myself   Delegate

Overspend on elaborate, expensive gifts	Make meaningful, low cost gifts/ give gifts of time
Give gifts to only family members	Give alternative gifts to those in need
Cook an elaborate dinner	Simplify, pick up a ready-made, grocery-store-dinner serve a Christmas meal at a shelter
Send lots of cards	Send form letter/cut list/eliminate
Devote every possible moment to Christmas activities & preparations	Emphasize meaningful activities
Emphasize Santa	Focus on the true spirit of giving (St. Nicholas Day, December 5) and the birth of Jesus
Obsess about getting errands done	Spread goodwill, compassion and cheer
Overeat, skip exercising	Eat healthily, exercise regularly
Contribute to family squabbles	Vow to discuss family issues in a civil manner
Frantically make it through the holidays	Enjoy the holidays, focus on the true meaning!

| Become obsessed with making everyone's holiday an extravaganza | Plan so that the entire family, as well as others, are truly warmed by a spirit-filled, meaningful Christmas. |

Forming good goals can help with your tradition changes. The following are a few suggestions to Assist you in writeing your own:

- I want to minimize Christmas preparations.
- I want to emphasize the true meaning of the season.
- I want to simplify my gift giving/give more thoughtful gifts.
- I want to spend more relaxed time with my children.
- I want to schedule uplifting concerts and productions.

_____
_____
_____
_____
_____
_____
_____
_____
_____
_____
_____
_____
_____
_____
_____
_____
_____

Be Specific

Next, be specific. If you want to emphasize the true meaning of the season, how will you accomplish that goal? If you plan to give alternative gifts, describe what type of gifts you have in mind. Will they be in the form of checks written to charitable organizations? If so, which ones and how much? If they are gifts you will be making, what sort of gifts will you make; where will you get the supplies; how much will they cost; how long will it take you to make them? If you have a game plan for Christmas giving, you are much more likely to succeed and will most likely emerge from the season with a more fulfilling feeling towards gift-giving (and probably leave everyone more pleased with their specialized gift.)

If you want to attend more concerts, dramas and plays, how will you discover the offerings in your town and vicinity? Will you include the children? Which ones are appropriate for them? How will you prepare them for what they will see and hear?

CHAPTER 3

TRADITIONS TO TREASURE

In chapter 2 you evaluated your outmoded traditions and hopefully did some reevaluating. Below are some specific ideas to spark your individual creativity. Give them a unique twist and you're on your way to beginning new traditions – traditions to treasure!

Focus on Hospitality

Focus on using your gift of hospitality when welcoming guests instead of merely entertaining them. In so doing, the warmth of fellowship takes precedence over a perfectly appointed and decorated home.

Open your celebrations to those outside the family circle. I fondly recall inviting a couple to our home for Christmas dinner. Our daughter and son-in-law had met them on the ski hill. They were alone and had planned to see a movie on Christmas afternoon. Instead we made new friends with this Jewish couple Shared our devotions about the true meaning of Christmas.

Change Gift-Giving Traditions

Friends and relatives may initially resist suggestions to change your gift-giving traditions, but once they experience the joy of a more creative way of giving, chances are they will become as enthusiastic about this innovative twist as you are. When dealing with small children, proceed with caution. Mutiny and downright anarchy might be the result if you propose a Christmas of giving only to the needy in your community and eliminating the gifts to them.

Family and friends might not automatically agree with your plans; we are a culture that has been brain-washed into commercializing Christmas. I suggest a gradual yet persistent change to a more Christ-centered celebration. Large numbers of Americans want simpler, more spiritual celebrations of the Christmas holiday. Tell your family that you're not giving up on traditions. Instead, instill in them the possibility that there is a way to celebrate so that Christmas becomes a more joyous and meaningful celebration.

You might want to enlist others in your plans for a merrier Christmas. One way is to download "Christmas Gift Exemption Vouchers" from the Adbusters Web site, which exempts the recipient from buying you gifts, conditional on them spending quality time with you instead. If they are likely to be lighthearted, you may want to send them the annual newsletter of SCROOGE, the Society to Curtail Ridiculous, Outrageous, and Ostentatious Gift Exchanges. If they're more solemn, the *Alternative Celebrations Catalogue* from the Christian group "Alternatives" might be appropriate.

Adbusters can be found at www.Adbusters.org; SCROOGE is located at 1447 Westwood Road, Charlottesville VA 22903; the address for Alternatives is P.O. Box 429, Ellenwood, GA 30049, phone 404-961-0102. See Chapter 8 for other alternative gift-giving suggestions.

Focus on Seeing God in People, Places and Things

Children love to be involved in observing and discovering. A way to practically implement this at Christmastime and at the same time heighten the spiritual drama of the season is to have children observe places they see God at work. When they see a friend help a schoolmate with a project, receive an unexpected gift, hear a stirring anthem, or observe the beauty of a snowfall, they can record it in the Holiday Events Diary in Chapter 10.

Become Secret Angels

One way to help children appreciate each other and to encourage acts of kindness toward one another is through the secret angel project. "During this season," says Kathy Van Dam, "we look for and serve the Christ in others. We try to form the habit of thinking of others before we think of ourselves". The Kurt Van Dams best implement this by becoming "Secret Angels" for the four weeks before Christmas.

"As the secret angel," says Kathy, we look at things in the same the way that a real angel would look at them. The object is to become an 'angel' and to treat the secret family member as an angel would treat us, with love and respect."

"I love doing this," bubbles 12-year-old Diane Van Dam. "It makes me feel so loved to have someone think about what I might need. I really like being the one who is doing secret good deeds. It makes me feel so good."

"I think it sets the right mood for the season," says Kathy, eyes glowing. "It teaches our four children the love of giving and the importance of serving one another." [1]

How to initiate the secret angel practice:

Put each family member's name on a slip of paper; each person secretly chooses a name. The person whose name is chosen receives acts of kindness throughout the season from that family member. The secret angel reveals his or her identity at a given time, perhaps at Christmas morning. This could be done by putting the "angel's" name on a slip of paper and tucking it under each family member's plate.

Prayer for Serving Others

Dear Lord, please show us how You would have us serve others this Christmas season and empower us as Your vessels that, by serving others, we may bring You glory. Amen.

Secret angels do acts of kindness for family members.

Benefits of Acts of Kindness

When I observe someone being kind to another person, there are three simultaneous benefits. The person receiving the kindness feels cared for and valued. The person expressing the kindness feels the joy of giving, and of having a positive impact on another's life.

But there is a third beneficiary of this encounter – me! When I observe an act of kindness, love and hope spring up in me. As I watch the interaction between the giver and receiver, I too am blessed.

With this in mind, I choose to uplift others. I demonstrate kindness, consideration, compassion, and patience – gifts from the heart – knowing the effects ripple out to bless unseen others.[2]

Recite the Christmas Story

You might encourage your children to memorize the Christmas story from Luke 2. It could become a tradition to recite the story from memory on Christmas Eve or Christmas Day. Instead of plunging into gift unwrapping, pause to remember THE GIFT and give thanks for the reason for the season, the greatest Gift of all!

Recreate the Christmas Story

Many families enjoy creating works of art together. You could put your budding artists to work creating a mural on shelf paper depicting the story of Jesus' birth with colored pencils, markers or crayons. Younger children might want to tell the story through use of recycled Christmas cards. Each card becomes a cue to the telling that segment of the story.

Reenact the Christmas Story

My friend, Cathy Bouws, helps her grandchildren bring the Nativity to life. She begins with appropriate costumes for everyone. Cathy has bought the costume clothing online at a costumes website and also purchased it at a second-hand store. Bathrobes are perfect for Joseph and the wise men; paper crowns, either made from poster board or obtained from a fast food store, complete the wise mens' ensembles. Sheets tied with silver cords serve as the angel's attire and a glittery headband or coat hanger wrapped with white or silver angora or tinsel makes a perfect halo. Mary wears a long dress or large shirt tied with a sash, a shawl draped over her shoulders. A doll or stuffed animal wrapped in a blanket is a stand-in for the baby Jesus. The shepherds wear bathrobes or pajamas. Canes or yardsticks are perfect for the shepherd's staff. Any extra children become wooly sheep, adorned with a white wool sweater or fluffy bathrobe. The nativity story comes to life during the narration. Cathy reads the story from a book, *The Story of Christmas, A Nativity Tale for Children*, by Anita Ganeri. You could also read it directly from Luke 2.

Making a video of the production preserves the precious memories that can be relived from year to year and will be a record of the growth of each child.

Children enjoy reenacting the Christmas story.

Tell the Christmas Story to Children

When Nancy Whisman discovered her oldest son's first-grade class had spent an entire week learning about Hanukkah, she went to the teacher and asked if she could have time to tell her students the story of Christmas. She told the story of the Nativity through the use of a crèche that her mother-in-law had made for the family and allowed the children to handle it and ask questions.

Since that time, she has asked each of the children's teachers if she could come to tell the Christmas story. Many people pray for her before, during, and after the date of her talk.

Amplify the Christmas Story

This year I amplified Luke 2:1-14, doing research and meditating on each significant word or phrase. It was an interesting and unique way to digest the history and significance of the story of Jesus' birth. A copy of it was my take-home-gift to my Christmas Day dinner guests — so much more meaningful than chocolates!

Luke 2:1-14 Amplified

In those days, (the days when the Romans ruled much of the world, when there was relative peace known as the Pax Romana, and when there was one universal language...Latin... and the roads were built to all parts of the known earth) a decree went out from Emperor Augustus, (born in 63 B.C.; founder of the Roman Empire; born into an old, wealthy equestrian branch of the Plebian Octavii family, autocrat of the Roman republic as military dictator) that all the world, (the Roman Empire which included Cyrene, northern Africa, Spain, southern Europe, Turkey, Crete, Phoenecia, Syria, Assyria and Babylon) should be registered (a census taken.) This was the first registration and was taken when Quirinius (born 51 BC, a Roman aristocrat from Lanuvium near Rome; appointed legate of Syria. It was his duty was to conduct a census for taxation purposes. Censes were forbidden by law and this one triggered a revolt, led by Judas of Galilee resulting in the formation of the Zealots, a religious group who opposed the Roman government) was governor of Syria, (a country in western Asia, home to diverse ethnic groups including the Arab Sunnis which make up the majority of the Muslim population. The capital city is Damascus, and it is bordered by Turkey, Iraq, Jordan and Israel.)

All went to their own towns to be registered. Joseph, (righteous teenager who was engaged to Mary of Nazareth; he obeyed God by marrying his dear friend, despite the fact that he would be ridiculed by the public and shamed by not being allowed into the synagogue since he would be acknowledging his parentage of the illegitimate child by this act of marriage), also went from the town of Nazareth in Galilee, (the region east of the Sea of Galilee, Nazareth being at the south end of this province,) to the city of David called Bethlehem, (an 80 mile journey from Nazareth or 100 miles if taking the long route around Samaria to avoid problems with the outcasts of Israel; largest city in the north district of Israel made up of Muslims and Christians, and childhood home of Jesus. The name Nazareth comes from the word *Nezer*, meaning branch or shoot, which refers to the passage in Isaiah 11:1: A shoot will come from the stump of Jesse. Jesse was the father of King David, the second king of Israel following Saul's reign and from whose lineage the Savior was predicted), because he was descended from the house and family of David. His branch will bear fruit to Judea, the city of David called Bethlehem, (located five miles south of Jerusalem, today's population being 28,000, located in the West Bank and was the scene for the book of Ruth), because he was descended from the house of David (as was Mary).

He went to be registered with Mary, to whom he was engaged and who was expecting a child, (Jesus, the long expected Messiah). While they were there, the time came for her to deliver her child. And she gave birth (perhaps without assistance since men in those days were not allowed to assist in birthing) to her firstborn son and wrapped him in bands of cloth, and laid him in a manger, (a stone trough from which the animals drank – the One known as "Living Water" was laid in a *water* receptacle) – because there was no place for them in the inn.

In that region there were shepherds, (the despised outcasts of society) living in the fields (since they had to constantly watch the sheep who are dumb, dependent creatures) keeping watch over their flock by night. But the angel of the Lord, (Michael, the archangel), stood before them, and the glory of the Lord shone, around them, and they were terrified, (no doubt because the angel was so dazzling due to his amazing luminosity and awesome presence). But the angel said to them, Do not be afraid; for see, I am bringing you good news of great joy for all the people: (everyone, everywhere, through all time regardless of race, color, sex or creed), to you is born in the city of David a Savior, who is the Messiah, the Lord. This will be a sign for you: (so that you can easily detect Him) you will find a child wrapped in bands of cloth and lying in a manger. And suddenly there was with the angel a multitude (perhaps thousands!) of the heavenly host, praising God and saying, "Glory to God in the highest heaven, and on earth peace, (not world peace but peace of mind and heart and between you and your fellow men and women) among those whom He favors!" When the angels had left them and gone into heaven, the shepherds said to one another, "Let us go now to Bethlehem and see this thing that has taken place, which the Lord has made known to us." So they went with haste and found Mary and Joseph, and the child lying in a manger. When they saw this, they made known what had been told them about this child; and all who heard it were amazed at what the shepherds told them. But Mary treasured (continued to think about, not divulging her thoughts to anyone but Joseph and God) all these words and pondered them in her heart (thought about their meaning for her future and the rest of creation throughout time). The shepherds, (whose lowly status was greatly elevated that glorious day), returned, glorifying and praising God, (the gracious and merciful Father who descended to earth to grant us eternal life and give us a model for living rightly) for all they had heard and seen, (amazing events that would live in their memories forever) as it had been told them.

Enhance the Season's Joy through Productions

You might want to make it a habit each Christmas season to attend a drama or concert in keeping with the children's ages. Reverend Bill Boersma, pastor of Christ Memorial Church in Holland, Michigan, and his family have made it a tradition to attend a production of *A Christmas Carol* each year. Through *Scrooge,* this production presents a great moral to discuss - the blessing of giving, not hoarding, at another's expense. *The Hallelujah Chorus* is always soul-stirring for older children and adults. And *The Nutcracker*, either the ballet or drama, is a wonderful analogy of the Christmas story. You might want to read the book and listen to the sound track before seeing the musical and discuss afterward who each character relates to in the Biblical story (even the Spider has significance as John the Baptist who points the way to Christ for those who are lost!) Afterward discuss the significance of the performance. Ask questions such as: Did it honor Christ? Was it symbolic? Was it realistic? What was the most inspiring part? Why? How will it change the way you live? Would you like to see it again?

What Advent is All About

Advent is a season of the church year which begins four Sundays before Christmas. The word *Advent* originally came from the Greek word *parousia* meaning presence; the presence of Christ. It is also a time when we concentrate on giving, loving, making special things and caring for one another.

Now fast forward a few thousand years and we find the Latin word *adventus* meaning "a coming." Now we not only have the presence of the Lord on earth but an understanding of his arrival. The first time

21

the word *Advent* appeared in the English language was in 1099, over a thousand years after the death of Jesus.

Caroling to the Elderly

Bill and Sally Doebler of Holland, Michigan organize a group of friends to go caroling each year to the residences and nursing homes of elderly persons in the area who greatly appreciate the joy that this tradition of music brings to them.

At-Home Christmas Concert

One family, inspired by the father, Paul, reluctantly began a tradition. Paul gave an invitation to each of the children as well as his wife, Jan. It read:

You Are Cordially Invited

"You are cordially invited to a special candlelight concert of recorded Christmas music, 4:30-5:30 p.m., December 24. R.S.V.P."

The children, Jennifer, age eleven, and Chris, age eight, eagerly flipped theirs open and then looked disappointed. No one, including Jan, wanted to sit quietly for an hour on Christmas Eve!

Reluctantly they conceded, mostly to humor Paul.

Promptly at 4:30 the concert began in the living room, amidst a setting of softly glowing candles. The beautiful sounds of Christmas filled the air, from the *Messiah* to "Joy to the World," from choir to solo to instrumental. The busyness of the final wrap-up to the big day was hushed as the family sat watching the flickering candles send shadows of dancing light all over the room, quieted by the soft music proclaiming

Christ's birth. For three years the tradition has remained an integral part of the families' celebration.

One year Paul's parents visited them. They none too eagerly joined the others in the living room for an hour, which they planned to endure out of politeness. However, as they left for the airport two days later, Paul's father said, "I'll never forget that wonderful hour of music. I really felt the Spirit of God preparing me to celebrate Christmas."

Advent Wreath Making Simplified

One way to keep the true meaning of Christmas central is to construct an advent wreath. Each day of Advent a candle is lit (one for each week). It is up to you to decide what to do during the time when the wreath candles are burning. If your children are young you might choose to purchase some children's books to be read during this time or they may be checked out of the city or church library. There are also many wonderful devotionals that can be purchased at your church library, local bookstore or online to use for Advent family devotions.

The use of an Advent wreath can visually remind us that the revelation of God is not a series of unrelated events, but rather a process in which the lights that are lit, and the lessons that are learned are added to what has gone before, as we anticipate the light that comes into our sin-darkened world at Christmas.

The Advent wreath has become a favorite of many because its meaning can be customized by the family. There is no single set system, either Biblically or traditionally. Each year we can assign different words (hope, love, joy, peace) that are traditional, or names (prophets, shepherds, angels, wise men) to the candles and choose a theme that creates in our worship an increased awareness of the gradual brightening in the darkness of our lives.

One custom from which my husband and I never wavered when our children were young is that of constructing an Advent wreath, which we religiously lit during evening devotions.

How to make your wreath:

1. Purchase a foam wreath-shaped form (it should be made of the soft, porous type of florist foam).
2. Soak it in water at least ½ hour.
3. Cut fresh greens two to three inches long. Insert them into the wreath. Add berries or other decorations if desired. (Artificial greens can be substituted. Use a dry-foam wreath for this type.)
4. Insert specially designed plastic candleholders into the foam. Insert four candles into the wreath. (The candles are traditionally three purple and one pink, though other colors may be used).
5. Place on fireproof plate or tray. (Caution young children about fire safety).
6. Reserve four small white candles or use one large, white, Jesus candle for the wreath's center.
7. Discuss the candles' names:

> Love — purple
> Hope — purple
> Joy — pink
> Good news — purple
> Jesus/Christmas — white

Candles are a beautiful, traditional reminder that Jesus is the Light of the World. They also serve as a visual aid which adults, as well as children, appreciate. They add importance and festivity to a celebration. If the advent wreath is not used, four candles set in holders will serve as well.

Discuss the format of the devotional, whichever one you choose to use.

Light the first candle (love — purple) for a week beginning the first Sunday of December. Light one more candle each week until all four are lit. Discuss the candle names.

Family Bible Readings for December

These brief daily Bible readings take incidents from the story of the first Christmas for your family to think and talk about. You could use them each morning or evening as you light the Advent wreath candles or as the basis for your personal Advent devotions. Consider meditating on or journaling each day's selection. Perhaps these verses could even be memorized!

Begin on December 1 and read one passage a day, ending on Christmas Day.

Hundreds of years before Jesus was born, God's prophets, who foretold future events, said that He would come.

> **Day 1** Micah 5:2 — His birthplace
> **Day 2** Isaiah 7:14 — His virgin mother
> **Day 3** Isaiah 9:6 — Who Jesus would be

And then, finally, it was time for Jesus to be born.

> **Day 4** Galatians 1:26-28 — The right time!
> **Day 5** Luke 1:26-28 — An angel told Mary
> **Day 6** Luke 1:29-37 — and carefully explained
> **Day 7** Luke 1:38 — Mary said, "I'm willing."
> **Day 8** Luke 1:39-40 — Mary visited in Judea
> **Day 9** Luke 1:41-45 — Elizabeth was happy.
> **Day 10** Luke 1:46-55 — Mary praised God.

Mary was engaged to a man named Joseph. An angel told him about Mary being Jesus' mother.

> **Day 11** Matthew 1:18-23 — Joseph listened.
> **Day 12** Matthew 1:24 — He obeyed the angel and took
> Mary as his wife.

A little while after Joseph had taken Mary to care for her, the emperor said everyone must go to Bethlehem for the census.

Day 13 Luke 2:6 — Jesus was born!
Day 14 Luke 2:8-14 — Angels sang the news!
Day 15 Luke 2:15 — Shepherds hurried to see.
Day 16 Luke 2:17 — Then they told everyone.
Day 17 Luke 2:19 — Mary remembered all.

At the time Jesus was born in Bethlehem, Herod was king. Sometime afterwards men came from far eastern lands.

Day 18 Matthew 2:1-2 — wise men inquire about a new king.
Day 19 Matthew 2:3-8 — Herod worries about a kingship competition.
Day 20 Matthew 2:9-10 — Wise men find Jesus.
Day 21 Matthew 2:11 — Wise men worship Jesus.
Day 22 Matthew 2:12 — Wise men secretly return home.
Day 23 Matthew 2:13-15 — Joseph and Mary flee with Jesus to Egypt.
Day 24 Matthew 2:19-23 — Joseph, Mary and Jesus return to Nazareth.
Day 25 Luke 2:40 — Jesus grew strong and wise.

Your Advent wreath becomes the centerpiece for your daily devotionals.

A Birthday Party for Jesus

On Christmas Day, replace the wreath with a Bundt or circle cake, placing the large candle in the center hole in the cake. Then have a birthday party for Jesus.

Helium balloons would be a festive addition to your party.

Bundt cake recipe:

Ingredients:

1 cup butter, softened
2 ½ cups sugar
4 eggs
3 cups unbleached all-purpose flour or gluten-free flour mixture (see combination in Chocolate Zucchini Cakes, Chapter 8, Gift Giving Revisited).
¼ t. baking soda
1 cup buttermilk
1 t. vanilla extract
confectioners' sugar

Directions:

In a large bowl, cream, butter and sugar until light and fluffy.

Add eggs, one at a time, beating well after each addition. Combine flour and baking soda; add alternately with buttermilk and beat well. Stir in vanilla. Stir in chocolate chips or nuts as desired.

Pour into greased and floured 10-in. fluted tube or Bundt pan. Bake at 325 degrees for 70 minutes or until a toothpick inserted near the center comes out clean. Cool in pan for 15 minutes before removing to a wire rack to cool completely. Dust with confectioners' sugar. Serve with berries and/or vanilla ice cream. Yield: 16-20 servings.

Prophesies

Look up the Old and New Testament prophecies. On small pieces of paper print several prophecies regarding Jesus' coming to earth. Roll and insert the papers into the Bundt cake prior to baking. Each person who receives a prophecy gets to read it. Consider using these:

O.T. Prophecy		N.T Fulfillment
Of the tribe of Judah	Genesis 49:10	Hebrews 7:14
Of the family line of Jesse	Isaiah 11:1	Matthew 1:1
A prophet	Deut. 18:15ff	John 3:34
A priest, but not from Levi	Ps. 110:4	Hebrews 5:6
A judge	Isaiah 33:22	John 5:22
A king	Psalm 2:6	I Timothy 1:17
Anointed by the Holy Spirit	Isaiah 11:2	Matthew 3:16
Performed Miracles	Isaiah 35: 5-6	Matthew 4:23-24
Taught Parables	Psalm 78:2	Matthew 13:35

Alternately, on small pieces of paper, write the names of different virtues Jesus would appreciate such as patience, cheerfulness, honesty, faithfulness, helpfulness, or compassion. Push the papers into the baked cake before frosting it. The child who gets that particular virtue reads it out loud and tries to practice that virtue at least for the year, hopefully a lifetime.

Light the Jesus candle. After it has been lit, each family member holds a candle which he or she can light from the Jesus candle. (Insert the candle in a circle of heavy paper to catch wax drips). Turn down the lights.

Sing happy birthday to Jesus as well as some favorite Christmas carols. Some possibilities are: "The Light of the World is Jesus," "Amazing Grace", "This Little Light of Mine" or "Go Light Your World" by Kathy Tricole. (You might want to purchase the CD of one or all of these songs and sing along with it or be accompanied by a family member who can play a musical instrument).

Perhaps a child could read this litany aloud:

The one constant each December is Jesus, symbolized by the Jesus candle, reminding us that the True Light has come into the world and that the darkness can never overcome it! Just as Jesus is our light, so these individual lights symbolize His Spirit. Before Jesus ascended to heaven, He said to his disciples, "All authority in heaven and on earth has been given to me. Therefore, go and make disciples of all nations, baptizing them in the name of the Father and of the Son and of the Holy Spirit, and teaching them to obey all that I have commanded you. And surely, I am with you always, to the very end of the age." (Matthew 28:19-20)

Only we can continue that.

When Jesus ascended to heaven He appointed His Spirit to give us power.

The light of the world is Jesus! We are his disciples with all the privileges and power that He has gifted to us. It is up to us to carry His light to everyone we meet. If we, as Christians, let our light shine to others so that they may see Jesus in us and thereby come to know Him, we can be a blessing to others and a powerful force for God!

Blow out your candles. Read aloud the journal in which you recorded ways in which your family was a blessing to others this holiday season. You may want to continue this practice throughout the year. Sharing the ways in which you bring light to the world is an encouragement to others!

Adopt a Grandparent

Make a shut-in's holiday season complete (and perhaps your own) by visiting him or her with your children at Christmastime. You might want to invite him to join you for Christmas Day dinner and festivities. If you find that you are compatible you might want to visit him regularly. (Check with a local nursing home before you visit to be matched up if you do not know of an elderly person). You could read books of interest to him or play board games together. I vividly remember taking our 2-year-old daughter to the nursing home where my husband's grandfather, Henry Jurries, resided. His face would light up when she walked into the room.

Older people love to reminisce. Over time you might want to videotape the shut-in telling of his memories from childhood through adulthood. This would become a legacy, a treasure for future generations. (See questions to ask when telling life's story from *The Compassionate Congregation*, by Karen Mulder and Ginger Jurries, pages 33-36, or purchase a journal formatted to record life memories). Deb Moore is a woman from Michigan who is a personal historian. She helps write memoirs and then converts them into books. She can be contacted at 616-957-4264 or www.TheStoriesOfYourLife.

CHAPTER 4

CHRIST-CENTERED ACTIVITIES

Making Treasured Memories

Here are a few suggestions for activities that will hopefully draw your family closer together during Advent as well as infuse more meaning into the holidays:

- Attend concerts or pageants. The Nutcracker contains symbolism. Attend a children's Christmas concert or pageant.
- Go caroling or listen to inspiring music. Have a sing-a-long each evening of Advent using CD's or a musical instrument.
- Read a Christmas story or poem each night of Advent.
- Turn off the lights and eat a picnic meal around the Christmas tree. If you have a fireplace, scent the room by throwing orange peels into it. End the meal by roasting marshmallows in the fire and telling or reading favorite Christmas stories or discussing a favorite family Christmas.
- Read, recite, or memorize the true Christmas story from Luke 2.
- Celebrate St. Nicholas Day (December 6) by reading the story of St. Nicholas and leaving shoes outside the door for him to fill on the night of December 5.
  (See Chapter 3 — Traditions that Inspire, also st.nicholascenter.org).

- Give each person at the dinner table an unlit candle to begin a round of grace. As they light the candle of the person next to them, they can say a simple blessing to pass along, such as "Peace be with you" or "May God bless you this Advent with His presence." Each person lights the candle of the next person, passing the blessing around the table until all the candles are lit. Conclude by singing a grace together such as, "The Lord bless you and keep you/the Lord make His face to shine upon you/ and give you peace/and give you peace. Amen."

- Make Christmas cards and bake cookies. Deliver them to nursing home residents or an elderly or sick neighbor. Sing Christmas carols to the residents.

- Write a letter from the heart to a friend or family member, giving thanks for some of the special things he or she has done for you over the years.

- Give coupons announcing service gifts: a back or foot rub, dinner at your house, teaching a skill, reading a book for an elderly person.

- Join with friends to become secret angels to the children of a needy family. Shop for and wrap gifts as a family, then leave them on the needy person's doorstep, ring the bell and run (ding-dong ditch-it style).

- Volunteer to serve dinner at a shelter during the holiday season.

- Make a family video interviewing all members about their memories of certain events or stories of family history; give each family involved a copy of the video.

- Make a family video each year with everyone singing the same carol or Christmas song such as *The Twelve Days of Christmas*. For those who are not musical, simply sing along to a familiar carol on a favorite CD. If you are musically talented, you might want to write your own lyrics to the tune of a well-known Christmas song.

- Plan and present a drama for shut-ins in the neighborhood.

- Put a box in your children's toy room and ask them to fill it with toys they no longer play with to bring to the Salvation Army or other service organization.
- Make pies for the city mission.
- Make pot holders. Sell them and use the money for needy children.
- Bring shoeboxes wrapped as a lift-open gift. Inside place a toy, book, candy, soap, washcloth, toothbrush, toothpaste, shampoo, etc. Bring to a women's organization that helps women in transition.
- Bring school supplies to migrant children.
- Knit scarves for a church care closet.
- Knit or purchase mittens for the church mitten tree.
- Decorate a small artificial or potted Christmas tree to bring to someone who is ill or incapacitated.
- Stamp out a love message in the snow to someone who is ill or shut in. Alternately use food coloring in a spray or squeeze bottle to write a message in the snow.
- Volunteer to help decorate your church for the season. Encourage members to donate poinsettias to decorate the church and then have those members deliver them to shut-ins or widows after Christmas.
- Make a Christmas banner to hang in your church or home. Banners may include only symbols or the words HOPE, PEACE, LOVE, FAITH, GOOD NEWS.
  (The book *The Advent Jesse Tree* by Dean Meador Lambert contains rich Advent symbols).
- Do a creative family activity such as making a gingerbread house together.
- Do one thing every day that brings you and your family joy.
- Do one thing every day for a friend or stranger that will bring him or her joy.
- Invite a single person to join you at a concert or at your home for Christmas dinner.

- Take a tour around the neighborhood to observe Christmas decorations.
- Write a note to someone who has had a positive effect on your life. Thank him or her specifically for what he or she means to you.

Tabletop Good-Deed Tree

Consider purchasing a small tabletop tree on which to hang ornaments cut from sturdy colored paper. Different colors could be used for each child, encouraging healthy competition and heightening the excitement. Attach the ornament to the tree with a ribbon each time an act of kindness is performed. You might want to write the act performed on the ornament. Hopefully, by the end of the Christmas season it will be beribboned with "good-deed ornaments", a beautiful visual reminder of the joy you have brought to others throughout the Christmas season.

(See page 38 for suggestions).

Thoughtful deeds become the focus of Advent.

Pray for Others all Year

Card Prayers

I feel a bit of sadness when all the colorful decorations are taken down after the Christmas season has ended.

I have always loved Christmas because of what it signifies — the celebration of our Savior's birth. I find it difficult to throw out the beautiful cards that we receive from friends and relatives so I keep them in a basket on our kitchen island for weeks after the decorations have made their way to storage. One day I was lingering over the basket of cards, reading them one last time before depositing them in the trash. Since this is the only time of year I hear from some of these people, I feel that throwing them away disconnects me from these dear friends.

As I was pondering this dilemma, an idea pushed its way into my mind. Why not keep the cards, choose one each week and pray for that person or family every day for an entire week. It has become a wonderful way to stay in touch during the year. Sometimes, I even send a short note letting the person or family know that I prayed for them. The response can be heartwarming and it's a wonderful way to keep Christ's love burning all year.

Keep a Crèche Central to Christmas

Crèche is actually a French word meaning *crib.*

A manger scene can become a meaningful and central part of your Christmas decorations. Many lovely ones are now available in ceramic, wood, metal, glass and porcelain. The crèche can become a cherished family possession.

Consider using a crèche in a dramatic way to tell the story of Christmas to your children over a series of days or weeks.

- On the first Sunday of Advent put out only the stable.

- On the second Sunday add donkeys to the manger scene.
- On the third Sunday put the shepherds and their sheep some distance away from the stable (on a bookshelf or table across the room). Put Mary and Joseph in another location.
- On the fourth Sunday move Mary and Joseph closer to the stable/cave. Place the wise men in a distant location, perhaps in an adjacent room.
- On Christmas Eve bring Mary and Joseph into the stable, hang the star, and add the angels to the scene. After your Christmas Eve service, place the baby Jesus into the manger. Bring the shepherds to the stable and place them around the manger.
- Throughout the twelve days of Christmas inch the wise men and their camels closer and closer to the scene. Remove the shepherds, stable, and animals, leaving only Joseph, Mary, and Jesus. Time the arrival of the wise men to occur on Epiphany, January 6. (The wise men didn't visit Jesus until He was about two years old).

If you choose to keep your crèche "in motion" as an ongoing storytelling device, you may want to combine the movement of the various pieces with the lighting of the candles on your Advent wreath and perhaps the singing of carols. Light the appropriate candle for each week, and sing a Christmas carol as your children move the manger-scene figures into position. Ask each person to share what that character gave to Jesus. Perhaps you could use this time to share a caring act each family member has performed on that day or share something for which you are thankful.

Creative Ideas for Incorporating Crèches

1. Visit a live outdoor crèche scene.
2. Purchase a large, soft crèche with which small children can play.

3. Place a different figure of the nativity scene in front of each family member's plate at dinnertime. Ask each person to share what that character of the Christmas story gave because he or she loved Jesus. (For example, Joseph gave a home, shepherds and wise men gave time to travel to Jesus' house, angels gave praise, and Mary gave her body and love).

4. Make your own crèche from clay, wood or paper.

5. Dramatize the Christmas story, perhaps with friends, allowing the children to assume the roles of the characters. (See Become a Crèche, Acting out the Christmas Story, Chapter 4).

6. Bring a crèche to school and use it as a prop to tell the Christmas story. Some public or charter schools will allow you to do this.

7. Hide the baby Jesus and allow the children to find him on Christmas morning. The person who finds him gets to put him in the manger scene and receives a small gift or coin.

(See "The Origin of the Crèche", Christmas Trivia, page 89).

How to Make an Advent Calendar

You may want to make your own Advent calendar. This can be a fun activity for Thanksgiving Day while dinner is cooking or after the meal when everyone is ready for a quiet time. The following instructions will help you construct your personalized calendar:

• Prepare two pieces of paper identical in size and shape. Your advent calendar doesn't need to be square or rectangular. You may want to make one in the shape of a star or an evergreen tree. Make the calendar at least 8 ½ inches by 11 inches and preferably 11 inches by 14 inches.

• Help your child mark out the panels and perforate three sides of each one with a pin. You will need to make as many panels as there are days between the start of Advent and Christmas.

(When in doubt, start your Advent calendar with December 1 and have 25 panels). The panels don't all need to be the same size; some can be larger than others.

- Put the two pieces of paper together as you perforate so that the pin pricks on the top sheet show through onto the second piece of paper underneath.

- Instruct your child to draw a Christmas picture of his or her own creation on the top sheet of paper. As he or she does this, be sure to carefully outline the boxes made by the pin pricks on the second sheet.

- Discuss various symbols with your child and let him or her draw those symbols in the boxes on the second sheet. (For symbol ideas, see *The Advent Tree, Decorations for Children and Adults to Prepare for the Coming of the Christ Child at Christmas* by Dean Meador Lambert).

- Make one of the panels a place to put a picture of baby Jesus. You may want to cut this from one of last year's Christmas cards or just write the name JESUS in the panel. Be sure to mark on the top sheet of paper — the one on which your child is coloring a larger scene — the location of that final panel. Glue the two sheets together, around the edges only.

- Put numbers on the three-sided panels on the top drawing. Use a contrasting color or dark ink. (The numbers should be small and not distract from the overall scene). Place the numbers at random, if you so desire, but make certain that the panel designated for December 25 is the one with the baby Jesus behind it.

An Advent calendar is a reminder to yourself and a way to point out to your child that the real meaning of Christmas isn't what we see, taste, or experience in the world. We celebrate Christmas by remembering that Jesus desires to be born anew in our hearts, minds, and souls.

Alternately, write daily suggestions on small folded slips of paper. Then place the papers in small envelope pockets glued onto poster board, one for each day in Advent. Using magic markers number the envelopes and decorate them, as well as the poster board, with Advent symbols (star, stable, donkey, angel, wreath, etc.)

Here are a few suggestions:

- Help someone struggling to carry something.
- Comfort someone who is hurting.
- Make a new friend.
- Buy a token gift for a depressed friend.
- Phone or email someone to say "I care."
- Visit an elderly person who is a shut-in.
- Write a thank you note telling someone you appreciate him or her.
- Make your brother or sister's bed without him or her knowing who did it.
- Do a chore that is not normally your responsibility.
- Compliment someone.
- Phone or email someone to say, "I love you."
- Bring a toy that your child no longer plays with to the Salvation Army or a Christian resale shop.
- Reach out to someone with whom you have had a relationship problem.
- Offer to help someone with a project.
- Offer to walk the neighbor's dog.
- Collect neighbor's empty pop cans; give the refund money to a favorite charity.
- Hold the door open for someone who is pushing a stroller or carrying packages.
- Write a letter of appreciation to a teacher.
- Comfort someone who is lonely or sad with a card or small Christmas tree or wreath.
- Baby sit for a neighbor who has small children so that she can do her shopping or just get a break.
- Bring flowers or a food gift to a neighbor.

- Do something caring for someone who has been unkind to you.
- Teach someone a song or trick.
- Say a prayer for someone who is sick or in trouble.
- Read a story to a younger sister or brother.
- Pray for a missionary or minister.
- Shovel or sweep your neighbor's walkway or driveway.
- Select a letter to Santa from the pile of letters at the post office or select a name from your church. Make a holiday wish come true for a less fortunate child or family.
- Visit a nursing home.
- Share one thing with your family for which you are thankful each day.
- Invite a friend to attend a holiday performance with you.
- Go on a special outing — treat a friend, neighbor or family member to lunch, ice skating or a concert.

Begin using your calendar 4 Sundays before Christmas Day.

How to Make a Wreath

The ancient Celts hung wreaths, a symbol of the cycle of life, on their doors to encourage the sun's lengthening days. It was the early Christians who used wreaths to represent God's never-ending love.

Wreaths can be made from fresh or artificial greenery and decorated with small bells or ornaments and a bow. Tie small bundles of fresh evergreens together; tie them to a wire frame. Pinecones can be wired to a frame and decorated or spray-painted. Twigs, seashells or various ornaments can comprise or enhance a wreath. Just a bit of imagination and some attractive materials are necessary. Wreath-making is an activity the whole family can enjoy doing together.

Progressive Breakfast

If you have a lot of family members in your city, you might try a progressive breakfast where everyone meets at one home for juice to look at that family's gifts and wish them a Merry Christmas. Then the entire group moves to the next home for bacon and eggs, then on for sweet rolls and hot chocolate, coffee or cider.

Photo Memory Tree

Add delightful activity to your holiday dinner with the use of a photo memory tree. Photos could be hung with ribbons on a small artificial evergreen tree or a tree branch that has been placed in a container and secured with florist foam, sand or plaster of Paris. Guests and family members are given the opportunity to choose one or more photos from which to tell their memories of the event or occasion.

Each person shares a memory of the event depicted on the photo.

Question Box

To keep the conversation interesting and incorporate everyone's input during a meal, fill a box or basket with questions. Each person chooses a question to answer.

Question box examples:

- If, through the use of a time machine, you could travel back in time to briefly revisit any Christmas moment in your life, which one would you choose?
- Of all your friends and family members, which person do you think is best suited to play the part of Santa Claus? Why?
- How do you think you would react if you were visited by an angel?
- What is the best Christmas surprise that you've ever had?
- What makes a Christmas gift really special to you?
- If you won $5,000 the week before Christmas, where would you go on vacation?
- If you could invite any famous person to your house for Christmas dinner, who would you invite?
- If you had $10,000 to give to charity which one would it be and why?

For more conversation ideas see, *The Christmas Conversation Piece (Creative Questions to Illuminate the Holidays)* by Bret Nicholaus and Paul Lowrie.

After the Gifts are Opened

You've gone to church, opened the gifts, phoned the grandmas and grandpas, Aunt Lil and Uncle Joe and there is a sense of "what's next" in the air. This is the perfect time to break a piñata (a paper maché donkey or other animal filled with candy and small gifts). Each child is blindfolded and given a stick with which to whack the piñata until it breaks. Stand back while pandemonium erupts!

In one home it is tradition to start a new jigsaw puzzle. Others gather around a game board to challenge one another to Monopoly, Scrabble, Rummikub or other game. Perhaps your family enjoys ice skating, touch football or a walk around the block.

Singing Christmas carols is a wonderful way to unite the family and bring smiles to weary faces.

Planning ahead can end the day on an upbeat note.

CHAPTER 5

THE STRESS MESS...
CLEANING IT UP

Although it may seem like stress is a "normal" evil accompanying the Christmas season, good news is on the way! Stress can become a thing of the past, being replaced with a more joy-filled, calm and fun-filled feeling. Achieving this utopian goal, however, takes time and planning. There are ways it can be done.

Sometimes, because some of our past holiday activities or habits have become so ingrained, we need permission to do things that are healthier or safer for ourselves. Likewise, we do not need to do things that could add stress to our holiday activities.

Bill of Rights for the Holidays

- You have the right to decline party/activity invitations.
- You have the right to give creative gifts that are within your budget (see chapter 8, Gift-Giving Revisited, for thrifty alternative gifts).
- You have the right to say no to drugs, cigarettes, alcohol, and sugary treats.
- You have the right to have mixed emotions: happy, sad, frustrated, guilty or afraid.

- You have the right to ask for help and support from your church, service agencies, friends and family if you are in distress or feeling any of the above emotions.
- You have the right to solitude for reflection, introspection and prayer.
- You have the right to decline a ride with a drunk driver.
- You have the right to *delegate* holiday tasks (that means you do not have to do everything yourself).
- You have the right to *enjoy* the holidays!

Five Steps to Relieving Stress

According to Doc Childre, research shows that the amount of stress you feel is based more on your *perception* of a person, place or event, than on the event itself.

Childre recommends these five steps:

1. Take time out so that you can temporarily disengage from your stressful thoughts and feelings.
2. Shift your focus to the area around your heart. Now feel your breath coming in through your heart and out through your solar plexus. *Practice breathing this way a few times to ease into the technique.*
3. Make a sincere effort to activate a positive feeling. *This can be a genuine feeling of appreciation or care for someone or something in your life.*
4. Ask yourself what would be an efficient, effective attitude or action that would balance and de-stress your system.
5. Quietly sense any change in perception and sustain it as long as you can.

> *Five minutes out of your day can save you hours of turmoil, reactivity and just plain unproductive time!*

Childre also recommends these simple self-massages:

Five One-Minute Massages

Palming Rub your hands together until you create heat from the friction. Then press your palms over your eyes, allowing that handmade warmth to sink in.

Cheekbone press Inhale deeply as you press your fingers into the tops of your cheekbones just below your eyes. Press firmly enough to move the tissue but not to cause pain. Exhale and release. Repeat, moving your fingers in half-inch increments toward your ears.

Forehead press Place the fingertips of both hands on your forehead so that they are pointing toward each other. Using as much pressure as you find comfortable, move your fingers in straight lines across the forehead to the temples, as if smoothing away tension.

Occiput press Place the fingertips on the tip of your head toward the back, thumbs at the base of your skull (the occiput). Press your thumbs in and up. Apply as much pressure as you think comfortable and slowly work your thumbs up the back of your head.

Scalp relaxer Place all your fingers and thumbs on your scalp. Applying pressure, move the skin around without moving your scalp.

If you enjoy body massages and are looking for a therapist, contact the American Massage Therapy Association at 708-864-0123 for a listing of those in your area.[1]

Destressing Tips

ORGANIZE

- Post a large calendar on the wall and write each family member's activities on it as well as deadlines for mailing Christmas cards or letters, etc.
- Place party invitations, tickets for concerts, etc. in order in a folder on the desk or in a file folder.
- Pace yourself. Set deadlines for projects; divide them into manageable segments.
- Order and address Christmas cards or letters in October.
- Clutter jangles our nerves. Resolve to keep the house picked up throughout the holiday season. Enlist the help of family members to achieve this goal.
- When you need help with holiday chores, don't assume that family members will automatically clue into your needs. (No kidding!) When you ask pleasantly and are specific — lists are the key to this — family members will usually step up to the plate. Making projects a fun-filled family time (sibling competition and time limits) will increase willingness to help, especially if the experience is made more pleasant with cheerful, holiday music and rewarded with your appreciation and cocoa and cookies!

DECLUTTER

- Declutter your kid's toy areas by evaluating his or her toys together. Discard irreparable ones and donate those no longer age appropriate or no longer of interest to the Salvation Army or other second hand store. You will put a smile on a child's face on Christmas morning and at the same time clean up your clutter.
- Put Christmas cards in a basket for later perusal.

DELEGATE

- Divide and conquer. Ask each child to pick three things he would like to be responsible for or list tasks on separate pieces of paper, place them in a basket and let each family member take turns drawing. **A word of warning:** Don't expect the tasks you delegate to be done the way you would do them. There is no right way to do things and if you ever want a helping hand again, resist the urge to jump in and redo, or correct your helpers.

BARTER

- Trade jobs you don't enjoy for those you do. For example, you decorate a friend's home; she makes costumes for your kid's Christmas pageant. You bake cookies and pies; your friend addresses Christmas cards.

KEEP IT SIMPLE

- Whatever you are doing, ask yourself how you could do it more efficiently. When entertaining guests over the holidays, for instance, I employ a caterer rather than spending the day in the kitchen. Because this is not always financially possible, you might ask friends to bring a dish to pass. If you have out-of-town guests, resist the urge to cook all the meals yourself. There are some great take-out delis or *One Dish Meal* establishments where you can make up your own dish with prepared ingredients.
- One year I decided that I was spending too much time wrapping gifts so now I either have them wrapped at the store or pay someone to wrap them or simply use an attractive holiday bag.
- One year I discovered a very meaningful devotional book, *Preparing for Jesus,* by Walter Wangerin. Another year the ideal gift was the DVD, *The Christmas Star* by Eric Larson. I

purchased a large quantity online for everyone on my list. It was Christ-centered, gender nonspecific and helped enhance others' Christmas meditations and meaningfulness of the season. Another wonderful holiday book to give is *Why the Nativity?* by David Jeremiah. For a gift for an entire family, the DVDs *The Nativity, Christmas with a Capital "C", or How the Grinch Stole Christmas,* are ideal. The book or DVD of the latter has a marvelous message, presented in a delightfully humorous way that only Dr. Seuss could deliver — the realization that, "Maybe Christmas doesn't come from a store, maybe Christmas is a little bit more!"

STAY HEALTHY

(Engaging in pleasurable activities raises antibody levels and helps prevent viruses from ruining the holidays.)

- Play games. Rummikub is a favorite in our family.
- Ride bikes.
- Dance to upbeat music.
- Sing carols.
- Play Frisbee with the family dog.
- Walk.
- Do yoga.
- Go fishing.
- Go sledding, skating, or skiing.
- Take naps.
- Get a massage, reflexology, or pedicure.
- Take a long tub bath with candles and soothing music.
- Read a book, poem or hymn (*Then Sings my Soul,* by Robert J. Morgan is a wonderful collection of 150 of the world's greatest hymns and stories of their origins published by Thomas Nelson).
- Watch a movie or DVD.
- Listen to soothing music.

- Do at least one kind deed for another every day.
- Drink plenty of water.
- Keep sweets to a minimum; snack on veggies and fruits instead.
- Meditate, imagine yourself relaxing on the beach or wherever you feel peace- filled, or recite a favorite Bible verse or passage.

STAY POSITIVE

- List holiday negatives and devise a plan to turn them into positives.
- Concentrate on the people you love rather than those who accelerate your irritate-o-meter.
- Make dates with friends who boost your energy level.
- Don't let anyone rush you and, most certainly, don't give anyone the power to ruin your holiday. When you notice you're feeling hurried or upset, just stop. Sit down. Breathe. Enjoy the lights or nature. Take a walk or meditate.
- Don't let anyone else force you to conform to their holiday "rules."[2]

> Get in the habit of stopping everything to take a small break. One great way to recharge is to recite specific verses that produce calm. Copy favorite Bible verses on cards and keep them handy for those times when you need a soothing time out.

See Advent as a Journey

The holiday season is often synonymous with gluttony. Not only do we overeat but we usually overdo everything: drinks, decorations, tight schedules, relatives and friends, not to mention extravagant gifts. We have come to expect to be overextended in every dimension during the holiday season. And often, we feel overwrought by our own over-doing!

I have often heard friends say, "Next year will be different!" At times we forget that Christmas is a season and not merely a day. Often the church year calendar is overlooked.

As soon as we begin to celebrate the season of Advent, December becomes a journey toward Christmas Day, a journey toward a cave and an amazing birth.

The wise men were prepared for their journey to see King Jesus. Their mission was to present gifts and to worship Him whose birth was signified in the stars.

As you follow the star, take time to prepare for what you will witness at the journey's end. Along the way consider a gift to offer to the Christ-King.

A worthy gift will be the gift that Jesus desires most: the gift of yourself, presented by way of an Advent fast.

Advent is a good time to chart an alternate course:

- Shut off the input. Decide to abstain from watching T.V. or listening to the radio.
- Decide to spend more time indoors and less doing errands and busy work.
- Shut yourself away, even if it's just for a day. Take extended time for prayer and meditation.

Why Fast?

Why engage in a physical fast at the start of the holiday season? Apart from the obvious counterattack on weight gain, here are some good reasons:

- A physical fast heightens your sense of taste. It allows you to re-enter the world of eating with a new appreciation for the taste of foods, especially the uncombined and unseasoned tastes of fresh fruits and vegetables.

- A physical fast causes your body to feel satisfied with less food. You will likely find that you feel less sluggish.
- A physical fast strengthens your own willpower, giving you a sense of power over your own eating habits.
- A physical fast heightens your other senses, as well as that of taste. Don't be surprised if holiday lights seem brighter to you, the colors of the season enhanced, the smells more vivid, the textures more luxurious.
- Finally, a physical fast heightens the entire Advent feeling of solemnity and reflection. A sparseness of eating is a good accompaniment for starkness of soul.

What Kinds of Fasts?

An early Advent fast may very well be a fasting from food. Consider setting aside at least a day for limiting your intake to water or unsweetened fruit juices. Allow your body a moment of respite; consider this to be a time for cleansing for your physical system.

You may want to fast from morning to night for several days. You may choose to limit your intake to certain types of foods. You might designate the entire Advent season as a time for abstaining from liquor, sugar, or high-fat foods.

If you are addicted to caffeine, nicotine, or any other chemical substance, Advent is a good season to recognize the hold that these chemicals have over you and to seek help.

A consultation with your physician before embarking on any type of fast is a good idea. Nearly every person, however, can choose to limit his or her intake or choices as a type of fast.

A Quiet Day

A Quiet Day is a fast, of sorts, from other people.

You can create your own Quiet Day. The elements of a Quiet Day are fairly common from group to group, and from person to person.

- *Establish quiet.* No television. No radio. No conversation. No music. The most purely defined Quiet Day is a day of fasting for the ears, a day without noise or input of any kind. Do not even talk to yourself, and offer only limited vocalized prayer.
- *Establish solitude.* This is your day to be alone. It is not a family day or even a day to share with friends or spouse.
- *Establish rest.* This is not the day to clean the house, run five miles, or finish a craft project. A Quiet Day is a day of rest for your body.
- *Establish contemplation.* A Quiet Day is a day for the soul. It is a day intended for fasting from the world with the purpose of spending time with the Lord. It is not simply a day of turning off the noise, activity, and routine of the world. It is a day for turning from the world to heaven.

Have a Silent Night

Dr. David Jeremiah suggests a radical idea for enhancing your Advent devotional time:

"In planning for Christmas this year, schedule a 'silent night' into your calendar.... Repeat Samuel's prayer: 'Speak, Lord, for your servant is listening' or David's prayer: 'Open my eyes, that I may see wondrous things from Your law.' (1 Samuel 3:9; Psalm 119:18).

You might read through the Christmas passages in the Gospels of Matthew and Luke or through the book of Colossians, listing all the attributes that describe Christ. List any Bible verses you would like to memorize.

Let this be your Christmas gift to the Lord Jesus, something that costs something in time and attention, but will end up giving you a fresh heart where all is calm and all is bright."[3]

Be a Peacemaker

What better way to de-stress Christmas than to be a peacemaker within your circle of friends and family.

Consider the following:

- **Verse to Remember:** "Do everything possible on your part to live in peace with everybody." Romans 12:18
- **Question to consider:** With whom do I need to restore a broken relationship this Christmas?
- **Point to Ponder:** We feel better about Christmas when we find a way to reach out to others. Ask yourself, "How might I do that?"

Families in Early Recovery Face Extra Stress during the Holidays

If Webster wanted to define the holiday season in ten words or less, this would probably do the trick: "A period of high stress caused primarily by unreasonable expectations."

Who hasn't felt the pressure to spend more than we can afford, to put up with unruly family behavior, to ignore uncomfortable feelings so we "won't ruin everyone's time" or take responsibility for the family's happiness? No wonder use and abuse of alcohol and other drugs increase during this time of year!

Families with someone in early recovery (less than two years) face these same problems but encounter some additional ones as well:

- High levels of tension, anxious or awkward feelings
  On top of the stress most of us feel during the holidays, people in early recovery experience powerful emotions numbed for years — like resentment, fear, shame and remorse. Family members finally express frustration and anger built up over a long time. Financial difficulties resulting from years of alcohol/drug abuse can make it hard for recovering parents to provide their families a "storybook Christmas," so it's easy to compare themselves to more fortunate families. All of these factors can lead to depression, self-pity or other feelings that are difficult to manage even at the best of times.

- Unreasonable expectations of how the holidays will be this year
  Finally released from active abuse of alcohol and other drugs, some families in early recovery hope that "this year will make up for all the bad years" or that "this year we'll be like those of other families" — in other words, pretty much perfect. This places significant pressure on every member of the family at a time of year when tensions are already high.

- Impatience with the progress of early recovery
  Families in early recovery often expect substantial changes quickly — putting additional pressure on the recovering person. Today's more potent drugs alter the user's body chemistry significantly and take a long time to reverse, while patterns of thinking and behavior for years can't be rebuilt overnight. Impatience can actually slow or block the desired changes.

- Subtle sabotage of recovery
  Families are fearful of difficult emotions heightened during the holidays. Others may question their whole purpose in the family. Even during the worst times, the addict/alcoholic seemed to need family members to care for, rescue, or cover for them. What is the family supposed to do now? Are they still even needed? This new role can lead to insecurity and subtle, even unconscious sabotage of recovery. Today treatment professionals have found certain steps useful to families moving into their

first holidays in recovery. The same principles can be helpful to any family during the holidays.

1. Keep clear that at the bottom line, drug and alcohol abuse is not acceptable in any form, no matter what the emotional state of the family. Period. It's essential not to surrender to the problem.

2. Put together a holiday plan. Assume things will be stressful. How exactly will you handle it without drinking? Do relatives really have to stay with you? What about that nice bed and breakfast nearby? Perhaps they could stay there instead of with you. Who's really stopping you from taking time for a short walk or a quiet half-hour alone when things become overwhelming?

3. Check your budget and agree on how much you will spend in advance for gifts, decorations and entertaining. Work it out before you go to the mall. Write it down!

4. Add support. If you have a family counselor, schedule additional sessions during December — regardless of how things feel now. Encourage the recovering person to go to more AA or NA meetings. Family members can benefit from attending Al-Anon or Al-a-teen meetings as well.

5. Expect some uncomfortable emotions from both the recovering person and family members. Try to be patient without "cosigning" abusive or destructive behavior. Most families encounter difficulties during the holidays. One way some families keep balanced perspective is to dedicate a time of day they share a few simple things for which they're grateful.

6. Consider a family "Giving Get-Together," where you all volunteer at a soup kitchen, homeless shelter, or senior center. Opportunities abound, and few things can make you feel as grateful for what you have than helping others who have less.

Whether it is company parties, difficult relatives, crowded malls or a maxed-out MasterCard, no time of the year compares with Thanksgiving to New Year's Day for stress. When you add the additional challenges facing a family in early recovery, it's easy to see why it's so important to have a plan in advance with reasonable expectations. Using some simple tools, it is possible for that first holiday season in recovery, while not perfect, could be much, much better than it has ever been before.[4]

Chapter 6

A Guide to Managing Holiday Grief

Anyone who has lost a loved one will attest to the special place grief has when celebrating the holidays. It is a time when families unite, feast together and have fun as they renew traditions, unless you are grieving the loss of a loved one. All the memories come flooding back, huge reminders of good times that will never be there again, or at least not in the same way. In the case of widows or widowers, there is the stab of loneliness whenever families are viewed having a good time together. In the loss of a child there is the empty stocking hung by the fireplace, painful reminders of the precious life now gone.

Blue Christmas Celebration

Some churches hold a *Blue Christmas* celebration to honor the memory of a deceased loved one. The following is a sample of a service that was given at the outset of the Advent season at Christ Memorial Church in Holland, Michigan.

    Welcome

    Prayer

Solo: *God Weeps with Those Who Weep*

Litany

O God our Help in Ages Past, sung in unison

Message/scripture: Romans 15:13, 5:5

Solo: *Appalachian Carol*

A Ritual of Reflection

Lighting of Candles of Remembrance/Place the name of loved one in basket*

Scriptures of Comfort

Praying our Goodbyes

Be Still My Soul/O God our Help in Ages Past, sung in unison

Benediction

Postlude

Each participant is given a candle and a card printed with the wording below:

The card may be put into a container and the rest of the service continues as participants stand in a circle holding their candles.

(Distribute copies of the songs to be sung.)

For you, _____,
who graced my life for a time, for hope of the life
ahead of me, and for trust in the power of God to
strengthen me, I light this candle in your honor and
with the hope of eternal life.

He will wipe away every tear from their eyes.
There will be no more death or mourning or
crying or pain, for the old order of things has
passed away. Revelation 21:4

Participants are invited to stay as long as they would like following the service. Refreshments are served and resources are available. The prayer room may be open and counselors from Hospice with lapel ribbons may be available to pray with participants.[1]

Handling the Holiday When Grief is a Visitor

When faced with the loss of a loved one, we are forced to make a decision to help ourselves move through the pain. The holidays increase the pain because they reverberate with the absence and the death of our child or sibling or mate. We are challenged to seek direction on just how we will endure the next few weeks.

The following are suggestions for you to ponder.

- Decide just how much holiday you can or want to handle. You can eliminate or modify all or some of your past holiday traditions such as holiday cards or decorations. Shopping need not be done if you lack the energy. If you feel the need to give a gift, then try cash or a gift certificate.

- Eliminate unnecessary stress—you need some special time for yourself. Avoid people who will add stress. Some have referred to these kinds of people as "toxic" people. Ask yourself the question, "Who are the people I feel most safe with?"

- Decide not to hide your grief. If the situation arises, then speak openly of your grief — mention the name of your child or sibling (or spouse). Most around you will be avoiding the mention of your child or sibling's name. So put his/her name in your conversation.

- Many who are bereaved decide to do something very different on the first Thanksgiving, Christmas, Hanukkah — so different that the absence of the loved one won't be so obvious. For instance, try going to a completely different place. A spa or cruise is a luxury which few can afford but it is an opportunity to be with other people who may also desire company during the Christmas season. You may also consider going to another city with a single friend.

- Decide to plan ahead for family gatherings. Don't let others plan for you. *Do what is right for you!* Focus on what *you* need and want to do. You do not have to go where *everyone* else thinks you should go.

- Decide to embrace your memories—not avoid or deny them. Do not hold back the tears. Decide whom you can reach out to if the feelings of anxiety and loneliness become too overwhelming. Don't be fearful of acknowledging that you need someone to be there for you.

- Express your faith. Only attend religious services if you feel they will help you to cope better with your feelings.

- One of the last lines in the play, *I Never Sang for My Father* is spoken by the son as he drives away from the funeral of his father - *"Death ends a life, but never a relationship."* Your relationship with your child or sibling is still very much alive. For now it may cause you some pain, but in the end, it will be the source of your strength to survive.

- Remember the anticipation of the holiday is often harder than the actual day.[2]

Activities to Help Grieve the Loss of a Loved One

Choose activities from this list that will give you comfort and peace.

- Look at photos/videos of your loved one.
- Send off a biodegradable balloon with attached message.
- Visit a place that has meaning to you and your loved one.
- Watch a DVD that was your loved one's favorite.
- Sing songs that soothe the soul.
- Light a candle in the loved one's memory.
- Plant a tree, bush or flower, named for your loved one.
- Smell something that elicits pleasant memories.
- Go to lunch and tell stories to a friend of your loved one.
- Create an ornament reminiscent of your loved one to hang on the Christmas tree.
- Read a special poem.
- Find a place to shout (and celebrate) your loved one's name as loudly as possible.
- Go for a walk and find a rock that symbolizes your love for you loved one.
- Think of something you are ready to let go of such as anger at someone or guilt. Build a fire, find a pinecone, and toss it into the fire to "burn up" the anger.
- Say a prayer telling God your feelings.
- Write a poem, draw a picture, or write a story about your loved one.
- Using your loved one's name as an acrostic, write a characteristic of your loved one with each letter.
- Using some of your loved one's clothing, make (or have someone make), a quilt or bunny or bear.
- Read the book, A Severe Mercy, by Sheldon Vanauken to read of ways that he productively grieved the tragic death of his dear wife.

Chapter 7

What to say?
What to do?

The Santa Dilemma

The mixture of Christmas can be confusing to children. On one hand, the Christian church emphasizes Joseph, Mary, and Jesus, along with the Magi and the shepherds. On the other hand, secular folklore has Father Christmas, *Pelznickel, Krampus,* Santa Claus, and Rudolph the Red nosed Reindeer. Which figures will children believe in? Since believing gives meaning and structure to childhood and since children gradually structure their lives on these beliefs, it is important to make wise choices. Santa Claus or Jesus, which figures will children believe in? Since believing gives meaning and structure to childhood, and since children gradually structure their lives on these beliefs, it is important to make wise choices.

Ask any small child the question, "Is there a Santa Claus? And you'll be greeted with shocked eyes. Ask any teenager the same question and eyes will roll heavenward. Clearly, somewhere between childhood and adolescence, a dreamlike shift in perception takes place. Is that good? Is it bad?

Ask these same people the question: "Is there a St. Nicholas?" and your answers will vary a lot more. Rarely will anyone fail to recognize the name itself, but since his Christmas role varies so much from country to country, synthesis is difficult to achieve.

Even more confusing to most people are these questions: "Who is the true St. Nicholas?" "Is he the same person as Santa Claus?" "Are all his European counterparts the same person?" Is there a *real* St. Nicholas? Or are they all mythical"?

Is it any wonder that so many of us are confused about who is real and who is not? How do we separate the genuine from the fake? Is there an original who deserves to be first among all these peers?[1]

The History of St. Nicholas

Yes, there really was a St. Nicholas, who the Dutch know as Sinterklaas. The old saint is unquestionably accepted into the hearts of all Dutch people and has been for centuries, yet one cannot help but wonder about his true origin, importance and place in history. In actuality the Nicholas' legend is at least 1500 years old and stems from two real bishops, Nicholas of Myra and Nicholas of Pinora, both living and dying between 241 and 546 A.D. (after Christ) in the area of Lycia in Asia Minor. While little is known of Nicholas of Pinora, Nicholas of Myra is known to have been born to wealthy parents in Patara, Lycia about 241 A.D. but was left an orphan at the age of nine during an epidemic sweeping his home city. Following this incident, the Christian church took Nicholas under its protective wing and in return he decided to give most of his family's fortune to the poor. As Nicholas grew into manhood, he became very popular with both the church and its neighboring townspeople. He became a young bishop in the early Christian church in Myra, now called Demre, Turkey and news of his many deeds and saintly behavior began to spread far and wide. As a result of this, many legends are still preserved today in painting, books and symbols. Soon after Nichols' death, which is recorded as December 6th, 342 A.D. the church and townspeople elected him to sainthood. He was buried within a church bearing his name.[2]

Legends of St. Nicholas

History brings us many a tale from the past adventures of the good St. Nicholas... Many of these legends have been preserved with the credit given to Swarte Piet (*black Peter*, his helper) for preserving them.

The most popular story is that of the poor peasant man with three daughters. Each of the girls was in love and wanted to be married, but their impoverished father was unable to provide the dowries (money required to contribute to the marriage) customary in those days. Each daughter was willing to sacrifice herself into slavery for the others. Nicholas overheard their tearful conversation and prayers one evening and resolved to return with an anonymous gift of gold coins in a purse. Nicholas left a purse of gold at their doorstep and naturally the family was elated. He returned twice more to deliver purses for each of the daughter's dowries. He tossed one in an open window and one down the chimney but was discovered by the father on the final delivery. Nicholas begged to remain anonymous and the father respected his wishes....

There are many more legends that recall the miraculous adventures of St. Nicholas but their details are obscure and basically unimportant when one considers the greater good of their mutual messages and prevalent theme: "It is in giving that we receive."[3]

From St. Nicholas to Santa Claus

On December 23, 1823 a poem appeared in the New York Troy Sentinel entitled, "A Visit from St. Nicholas". In the poem St. Nicholas is described as being chubby and plump with a broad face and a little round belly that shook when he laughed like a bowlful of jelly. Of course we know the poem as "'Twas the Night before Christmas", which was thought to have been written by Clement Clark Moore who claimed authorship 13 years after its publication. It is however purported to be more suited in structure and style to that of Henry Livingston Jr. so authorities lean toward giving him the credit but to this day it has not been proved either way.

The poem is significant in that it has influenced our transition from St. Nicholas as the patron saint of giving as a bishop who was trim, and who wore a red bishop robe and a mitered hat to a fat, fur-trimmed, velveteen suited benevolent personage whose sole purpose in life is to make and bestow toys to good boys and girls. Black Pete has been replaced by an army of green and red-suited elves.

Perhaps, instead of concentrating on the modern day fat fantasy fairy of fantastic gifts, or simply dismissing him as a commercial aspect of the season, it would be wise to emphasize his origins and the wonderful example of selfless giving which inspires us to do likewise, especially for those who are unable to reciprocate.

One mother decided to turn her daughter's curiosity about the authenticity of Santa around by encouraging her daughter to play "Santa." She suggested that she take two things off her wish list and give them to her friend, Maureen, who would otherwise not get any Christmas gifts. The idea of playing Santa energized Molly to change her focus to that of being a giver instead of a recipient and to anticipate the excitement of anonymously leaving the gifts along with a pair of shoes and a plate of cookies on Maureen's doorstep on Christmas Eve with a card that says, "Merry Christmas from Santa."

Molly's mother points out that the important thing about the encounter is not so much receiving the gifts as the fact that someone cared for her and was willing to show it.

She wisely shared with her the history of St. Nicholas and the connection to Santa Claus. Not only did she emphasize the spirit of Santa but also introduced her to the joy of giving so as not to destroy the fun of fantasy and wonder. She was also able to maintain her integrity by not deceiving Molly into believing a myth as truth. Children, of course, eventually discover the truth and then wonder about what other things the parents have been untruthful.

See website information about St. Nicholas in *Notes*.[4]

A Tale of Two Faiths

Sue and Ted Dykstra were from very different backgrounds — she Jewish, he Christian. The first time she met her future in-laws they were coming to the Dykstra house to celebrate Christmas. "I had never hung stockings, attended a Christian church service, tasted mincemeat, acknowledged Santa Claus, or in any way celebrated Christmas," recalls Sue.

After dinner that night Ted's mother asked Sue when she was going to light the Hanukkah candles. It was the first night of the Jewish Festival of Lights, when Jews light candles to commemorate the miracle of a small amount of oil that miraculously illuminated the newly rededicated temple for eight days and eight nights. She just assumed Sue would be celebrating her faith's holiday. Sue, on the other hand, imagined that if she observed Hanukkah, Ted's parents would be uncomfortable. She felt uneasy reminding them of their differences. "I quickly produced candles and holders for the menorah. Ted's whole family gathered around as I lit the tapers. Then I taught them to sing the blessing in Hebrew. We all trudged out to select a Christmas tree. Later, as the candles glowed in the window, Ted's mother taught me how to cut paper stars. These uniquely different activities have marked our holiday celebrations ever since."

Many families, like the Dykstras, believe that by celebrating Christmas as a religious holiday rather than a commercial one, their child will come through the December Dilemma toy-poor, perhaps, but spiritually rich.

"It's a conclusion we've been led to, in part, by our inability to celebrate by rote. The questions we must answer each December," Sue concludes, "aren't about what we will buy, and for whom, but about what we believe, and how we want to practice our faith."

The Jewish-Christian Marriage Dilemma

Nearly one million Jewish-Christian families live in this country and just the fact that problems can easily arise when a mixed-faith couple approaches the celebration of Christmas and Hanukkah has given rise to a name for this problem: the December Dilemma.

"Our children are grown up, but when they were younger, on Hanukkah, we gave family presents like jigsaw puzzles and games, things we could do together," says Mary Helene Rosenbaum, coauthor with husband Ned, a professor of Judaic Studies at Dickinson College in Carlisle, PA, of *Celebrating Our Differences: Living Two Faiths in One Marriage*. "Christmas is more religious," she says. "We go to Mass. We light the Advent wreath. It's not just presents and food, though it's that too."[5]

The Origins of Hanukkah

Have you ever heard the story of the origins of Hanukkah and the amazing connection to Christianity? If you do not know it, perhaps, after reading the story, you will decide to celebrate this holiday, no matter what your faith.

Two centuries before Jesus was born, Antiochus, a Selucid king was determined to Hellenize everyone (make them conform to the traditions, culture and religion of the Greeks.) This included the Jewish people. For these very godly people, the decree was like telling them to cut out their hearts, so devoted were they to serving God. They were forced to discontinue Sabbath worship, read the Toradh (their Bible) and circumcise their babies. They were instead commanded to worship several Greek gods.

Revolt was inevitable. In 168 B.C. Mattathias, from the Hasmonean family, led a resistence against Antiochus. Mattathias fled with his family to live in the hills. Other Jewish families followed and a community was settled. His son, Judah the Maccabee, led his people to victory in a three-year war with the Selucids. The victory was truly a miracle, an answer to many prayers since the Jewish people were incredibly outnumbered. (The ratio is compared to the state of Rhode Island going to war against the rest of the United States!)

Returning to Jerusalem, Judah led his people in a ritual to cleanse the temple, which had been desecrated by Antiochus. (He had sacrificed a pig — a forbidden animal to the Jewish people — on the altar and dragged the intestines all through the temple.) Antiochus had done this to discourage the Jews from worshipping there.

The temple was then rededicated. (Hanukkah is a Hebrew word meaning "dedication".)

Part of the cleansing ceremony included lighting an oil lamp for the 8-day period of cleansing. Although only a small amount of holy oil was left in the menorah, it was lit anyway. Miraculously, it burned for the entire 8 days! This was very significant to the Jews because, not only was it an amazing miracle, but also because the burning lamp symbolized God's eternal presence.

Each year about 2 ½ million people would stream into Judea to celebrate Hanukkah, also known as the Feast of Tabernacles of Light.

Jesus entered the outer court where, during the Feast of Tabernacles, four 86 foot high menorahs, each holding 65 gallons of olive oil, stood. On the last day of Sukkot, the Feast of Tabernacles, the giant menorahs were lit just as the sun was setting. 5,000 Levites led the people in chanting praises to God, accompanied by cymbals and drums. The fire was so great that millions of people all over Jerusalem who had come to celebrate the feast could see them. The menorahs represented the pillar of fire that led the people of Israel through the wilderness. It was in this context that Jesus, in a loud voice shouted, **"I AM THE LIGHT OF THE WORLD"**!

The feast is still celebrated by the Jews. Most Christians do not celebrate it, which is unfortunate since it was because of this victory that the Jewish race and religion were preserved so that Jesus, the Messiah, could be born.

How to Make a Menorah

Children could make their own menorah by following these instructions:

- Purchase 8 candles, any size, that will stand on their own.
- Purchase self-modeling clay.
- Line the candles side by side with about 2 inches between.
- Roll 2 lengths of the modeling clay until they are about ½ inch in diameter
- Weave one line of clay in and out of the candles so that the entire line of candles is encompassed; do the same thing with the second round of clay, weaving the clay in the opposite direction.
- Paint the menorah with bright colors when dry (perhaps the next day).

A menorah helps to mark the days in this historic miracle.

Celebrate Hanukkah

Hanukkah is called the Festival of Lights because it celebrates the miracle of the oil lamp. Lighting a menorah on Hanukkah is considered a mitzvah – a good deed. Your menorah can be shown in a window which is traditional. (Watch the news to discover on what day Hanukkah begins).

Hanukkah is celebrated for eight days. There are 8 candles, one for each day. There is also a service candle called the shamash which is used to light the other candles. Each night of Hanukkah a different candle is inserted in the menorah and lit. Begin lighting the candles on the right and work toward the left. The shamash remains in the center. The traditional colors are yellow, blue and red.

Do you have any Jewish friends or neighbors? Perhaps you could invite them to your house during Hanukkah for a celebration to tell them the story of the Jewish war with Antiochus and the Selucids and how it is related to Christmas. Many Jewish people do not know the stories behind their faith. Perhaps you could introduce them to your faith by inviting the children to dramatize the Christmas story. (See *Becoming a Crèche,* in Chapter 4, **Christ-Centered Activities**). Alternately the children could act out the battle against the wicked king led by Judah Maccabee. (Costumes could be improvised along with cardboard, foil-wrapped swords).

A part of this celebration is a traditional food called latkes, a shredded, fried potato pancake. One of the customs the Jews have during Hanukkah is to eat fried food since oil is used for the cooking process, a reminder of the miraculous burning of oil). Latkes are a favorite fried food. You may want to make these latkes before your guests arrive and fry them just before you are ready to eat.

Another favorite Hanukkah food is jelly donuts.

My First Hanukkah Board Book is a primer of Hanukkah information that young children might enjoy.

Children delight in acting out the battle between the Jews and Selucids.

Tasty Latkes

You will need:

> 3 medium potatoes
> 3 T flour
> 2 eggs, beaten
> ½ t salt
> sour cream
> applesauce
> vegetable oil for frying (olive or canola)
> zuchinni, carrot or beet (optional)
> colander
> grater
> strainer
> paper towels
> deep skillet

1. Preheat the oven to 200°.
2. Peel and grate the potatoes into a colander then to drain in the sink.
3. Mix the potatoes and onion together in a bowl. Stir in the flour, eggs and salt. Line a colander with paper towels.
4. Heat enough oil fry in a skillet. When the oil sizzles, drop latkes by tablespoons into the pan, leaving space between each. Flatten with the back of a spoon.
5. Fry each side until golden brown.
6. Use a spatula to place the latkes in the lined colander so that the paper towels can soak up extra oil. Then transfer them to an ovenproof dish and into the oven to keep warm while you make the next batch.
7. Serve with sour cream and applesauce or eat plain.

Questions:

Why did Mattathias revolt against the Greeks?

Who led the Jewish people to victory?

Why was the victory a miracle? Why did the temple need cleansing?

What miracle transpired when the oil was lit?

What were the containers of oil called?

Why is this miraculous event significant?

How do you think the people reacted when Jesus called at the top of his voice, **"I AM THE LIGHT OF THE WORLD?"** Do you think they all reacted the same way?

Chapter 8

Gift Giving Revisited

A New Look at an Old Custom

*You give but little when you give your possessions. It is
when you give of yourself that you truly give.*
Kahlil Gibran

What would Christmas be without gifts? This custom began in a
pure and unpretentious fashion. The wise men, as we know, presented
precious gifts to the Christ child. The gifts were appropriately symbolic
of the Christ (gold symbolized kingship, frankincense future priesthood
and myrrh the anointing oil of his kingship as well as his burial). The
gifts also, no doubt, financed the holy couple's flight into Egypt before
the horrible slaughter by Herod of all babies under two years of age.
This was his attempt to thwart the possible overthrow of his kingship
by a new child king. St. Nicholas became known for gift-giving when
he bestowed money to three women so they would have a dowry (the
money required to contribute to the marriage) thereby enabling them
to marry.

Gifts are a way to show our appreciation to friends and employees at
the end of the year. The giving of gifts has taken on a decidedly harried
hue, however, because of the way we have allowed this custom to run
wild. Children have been known to get the gimmies and circle every
toy in the catalogue or find the items online. We turn into animals

when there is a pre-Christmas sale or a limited amount of the hot toy of the season. We can't turn on T.V. without being bombarded with advertisements for every luxury, toy and gadget known to mankind. Then there's the rush in those last few days before the BIG day to find something — anything — just so we can have a gift under the tree (or in the mail). Have we all gone mad?

Perhaps we need to take another look at this custom gone awry which I refer to as "Excessmas".

I am a gift-giver to the core so I certainly don't recommend doing away with gifts altogether. What I am suggesting is that there be more meaning attached to our giving.

A wise sage once said, "The true measure of a gift is in its cost. Not the money you spend, but *the cost*. How much did you spend of your *love* and *caring*? How much thought went into it? How much *time* did you spend making it and/or adapting it to each individual?"

I will never forget the Christmas that I gathered photos, birth certificates, locks of baby hair and newspaper clippings of my husband's achievements and assembled all these momentos in a scrapbook. It was a huge project, taking many hours to assemble. I had as much pleasure in presenting it on Christmas Day as my appreciative husband had receiving it. I knew how significant a gift it was when one of our friends asked Jim what he had received for Christmas and the memory album was the only thing he could remember! (My children subsequently received these labors of love another Christmas).

Okay, so how would the new, transformed Christmas look in this vital area? What would we do differently so that the season becomes one we remember for its blessings, the gifts that transform and inspire?

Perhaps you could agree with friends and relatives that you will all comply with certain gift-giving rules:

1. gifts must be homemade
2. the gift must be a "white elephant" (something used that you no longer want)
3. a treasured book will be exchanged

4. the gift will be one of service
5. only gifts that emphasize in some way the true meaning of the season will be exchanged
6. gifts would be edible/grown in one's garden
7. gifts are to be demonstrated in some way: a drama, play, song, recitation (Biblical or otherwise), history of some aspect of the Christmas story, e.g., story of the star of Bethlehem, etc.
8. gifts of an experiential nature would be exchanged

Alternative Gifts

The following are some ideas for celebrating Christmas by giving unique gifts which are infinitely more meaningful than the store bought variety:

Gifts of Service

1. Write a letter recording your fondest memories of the times you spent together.
2. Create a video autobiography to give to family members who will appreciate having this bit of family history. (This can be done with a personal camcorder or by a professional. Deb Moore is a personal historian who helps people write their memoirs and turn them into books. Contact her for help with yours or a loved one's life story at www.TheStoriesOfYourLives.com or at 616-957-4264).
3. Do grocery shopping for a neighbor who can't get out of the house; promise to read books together; play your instrument at a friend's party; play games with a lonely neighbor; make home-cooked meals or cookies; paint neighbor's house; make a flower arrangement; knit, crochet or needlepoint a sweater or scarf, or anything that exemplifies your talent). Bring a decorated Christmas tree to an elderly or infirm friend.

4. Wrap a friend's Christmas gifts for him/her.
5. Offer to watch a neighbor's children for a morning or afternoon.
6. Clean house for someone who is ill or burdened with children or overly stressed.
7. Give a certificate to be redeemed for washing windows, shoveling snow, raking leaves or mowing the lawn.
8. Sew something useful such as a laundry bag, tote bag or flannel shoe caddies for travel.
9. Give a score of music you have written yourself.
10. Assemble a booklet of favorite recipes. (See page 81 for instructions).
11. Compile your favorite stories. Have them spiral-bound.
12. Plant slips from your garden.
13. Send a tree or bush.
14. Send a favorite magazine subscription.
15. Write a poem.
16. Calligraphy a friend's name with its meaning. (This can be done on your computer). Frame it.
17. Calligraphy a favorite verse. Frame it. Some suggestions: Psalm 23:1, Psalm 118:24, Prov. 16:24, Prov. 18:10, Prov. 21:21, Micah 6:8, John 10:10, Ephesians 1:17, Phil. 2:15a-16b, Phil 2:27, Phil 4:7, Phil. 4:13, Hebrews 11:1, I. Cor. 13:13, Rev. 4:8
18. Record a CD of your child playing a musical instrument for a relative.
19. Shovel a friend/neighbor's driveway.
20. Give computer lessons.
21. Drive to the store for a shut-in once a week.
22. Read to a shut-in from the Bible or a favorite book weekly.
23. Make a home-cooked meal regularly for a friend.
24. Walk your neighbor's dog regularly.

Gifts of Experience

Consider giving these gifts to be engaged in together:

- trip to a museum
- lessons on how to cook a dish, arrange flowers, carve something from wood, sew a quilt, etc.
- gardening expertise
- tickets to a concert, ballet or game
- holiday swag, wreath, or other decoration instructions
- tickets or note signifying a destination to go hiking, biking, snorkeling, or camping
- tickets to the circus
- gingerbread house kit to be baked and assembled
- lessons on how to paint a picture along with canvas or water color paper and paints
- bridge or tennis lessons
- favorite DVD to view together (see Resources that Make Memories, Chapter 12)
- relaxing CD (Deep Peace; Wine Country Sunset by Jack Jezro, guitar; Ocean Spa Flutes (*Quiet Time, Amalfi or Deep Peace*).
- coupons for weekly or monthly foot or body massage
- coupons for boat rides (charter or on your own)
- binoculars, bird book and a promise to go birding

Gifts from the Heart

Consider giving these thoughtful gifts:

- anonymous monetary gift or bag of groceries to someone who has recently lost a job, or is going through a hard time
- note to your pastor expressing your gratitude for his/her inspirational messages including a favorite CD

- letter to your parents or grandparents thanking them for some of the special ways they have affected your life
- restaurant coupons to someone who has just lost a spouse
- handmade gifts such as a flower arrangement, baked goods, nut mix, salad dressing, etc. (See recipes in Chapter 8.)
- candle to be lit each night of Advent and an Advent devotional
- journal with book, *One Thousand Gifts*, a beautiful little book about gratitude, by Amy Voskamp
- handmade stationery enhanced with a rubber stamp image or hand painted (special note paper is available at a paper store or Michaels for this purpose)
- found object such as a sea shell
- Christmas ornaments you no longer use
- homemade Advent calendar which can be custom made on your computer (see "Make an Advent Calendar", chapter 4, **Christ-Centered Activities**).
- *Bible* — choose from a number of versions or a contemporary translation, *The Message,* by Eugene Peterson
- favorite book recorded on a CD, to be enjoyed in the car or while exercising
- one of the many cherished Christmas books or DVDs. (See Resources that Make Memories, Chapter 12.)

Charitable Organizations

Helping Those in Third World Countries

At first, Mark Cameron had planned to take his sons to Hawaii for the holidays. The idea of sharing Christmas cheer surrounded by warm sands and crashing surf sounded wonderfully alluring. Instead, Mark, a vice president for the University of Phoenix in Salt Lake City, Utah, took sons Blake, 17, and Bryan, 11, to Garbanzo, Mexico. A tiny village at the end of a dirt road, Garbanzo is home to 80 impoverished souls who scratch out an existence growing meager gardens and herding bedraggled goats. In place of comfortable Hawaiian condos and dreamy palm trees, the Camerons found stone huts with dirt floors and no electricity. And they couldn't have been happier.

Ever since his brother had told him about a secular volunteer organization called the **Center for Humanitarian Outreach and Inter-Cultural Exchange (CHOICE)**, Mark had wanted to take his boys on a CHOICE expedition. CHOICE, a nonprofit agency based in Utah, leads small groups — including families — to villages in Vietnam, Mexico, Kenya, Bolivia, and Nepal. Volunteers help build schools and medical centers, and install water projects. They vaccinate animals, work in literacy programs and, if they are doctors or dentists, dispense health care.

While the Camerons had always been active in their church and community, this trip would be completely different, requiring a long and arduous journey from their comfortable home in the U.S. to the poorest regions of central Mexico. And it would change their lives forever.

For a week, the Camerons helped construct a foundation for a school building, hauling rock, mixing cement by hand, and laying brick alongside the villagers. "I've spent time with my children on family trips, but this was different," Mark says, "They weren't just focused on having fun, but on serving people."

At the end of the expedition, villagers and volunteers gathered for a farewell party. In Garbanzo, the villagers put on their finest clothes, and people rode horses over from neighboring villages. Under the moon and stars, far from any city, with the horses neighing and music playing, the Americans and Mexicans danced in the dusty roadways. "It was unlike anything I'd ever experienced," Mark says. "All the girls wanted to dance with my boys."

For more information on expeditions or to make a donation to help in its humanitarian work, contact: CHOICE Humanitarian, 7879 South 1530 West, Suite 200, West Jordan, UT 84088; 801-474-1277. Or try their web site: www. choice-humanitarian.org.

There are many other organizations offering travel and volunteer opportunities. Here are a few: www.ideallist.org — contains links to hundreds of non-profit agencies www.volunteerinternational.org — a great search site for volunteer opportunities overseas.

Water Missions International for cleaner water

This organization, begun and managed by George and Molly Green, makes large filters for disaster areas and third world countries for people who are dying of polluted water. Often these people do not know the cause of their disease. WMI's work is vitally important because 25,000 people around the world die *daily* of polluted, water-borne diseases. WMI makes possible the gift of clean water for thousands of people around the world. Contact them at: www.watermissionsinternational.org.

Goat Gifts

I am so touched by the mission trip that our friends, Doug and Mary Windemuller of Pine, Colorado have sacrificed to take. Right after Christmas several years ago they traveled to Rawanda, Africa with their grandson, Matthew, in order to purchase and distribute goats to some of the orphans and widows of the genocide. Pastors of local churches help identify recipients. They travel there under the auspices of CALM (Christian African Leadership Ministries). Each goat provides kids, milk, and fertilizer for the natives' crops. The first kid must be given to another widow and subsequent kids may be eaten.

My husband and I are excited about supporting this ministry because it is such a vital gift for poor widows. A little money goes a long way (one goat costs only $25) and only 10% of the donations are used for overhead. Money is also given to the widows for health care. A mere $5 provides health care for a family of 5!

Many people give notice of a goat purchase to a friend or relative for Christmas. Have you ever heard of giving a goat as a stocking stuffer?

To make a contribution for this worthwhile cause, contact www.calm.org.

Goats are delivered to widows in Rawanda.

Heifer International

Another animal-giving organization is Heifer International. The gift of a sheep, goat or chicken can help a family in a third world country sustain themselves. For instance, a dairy goat, is a lasting, meaningful way to help a family on the other side of the world. This gift can supply a family with up to several quarts of nutritious milk a day — a ton of milk a year. Extra milk can be sold or used to make butter or yogurt. Cost for 1 goat: $120. Contact **Heifer International at www.heifer. org** or call 800-422-0474.

Geegh Nursery School

Mary Geegh and her ministry are close to my family members' hearts. When my children were still young, a friend presented me with a book written by Mary entitled, *God Guides*. This treasure is filled with amazing accounts of Mary's guidance received by the Holy Spirit. Instead of giving these native people advice, she would give them pencil and paper and ask the Holy Spirit to provide them with a solution to their problems. He never failed to give the perfect wisdom for each situation.

Intrigued by this saintly woman, I made an appointment to meet her. She was so delightful and so humble that I brought my children, Kristin and Steve, to meet her. We would often visit her. She shared stories of her days in India and presented the children with treasures from that country. (My daughter, Kristin and her husband, Dave, currently serve as missionaries in Uruguay, partly because of Mary's influence!)

I have given over a hundred of her books to people in an effort to encourage them to listen to the Holy Spirit's guidance in all areas of their life.

In 1957 Mary started the Geegh Nursery School in Madanapalle, South India where she served as a missionary for 38 years. She began to notice that the children were left in the care of older siblings while their parents worked. The brothers and sisters would either miss school or take them along, often hindering their own education. Many of them would otherwise roam the streets, stealing goods in order to buy food. While serving as principal of the girl's mission high school, Mary sent one of the teachers outside to gather the little children together under a Banyon tree to sing Bible verses and prayer songs. Mary was challenged by the verse, "Lovest thou Me? Feed my lambs." John 21:15. This led to the development of a nursery school. The school started with 100 children who came from the poorest tribes in the villages surrounding Madanapalle. Daily they came to learn Bible teachings. Most of them became Christians and have led their parents to faith in Christ. Many have gone on to work in professions around the world. For only $10 per month, the program will provide an education, Bible studies, two meals a day, supplies, transportation, sewing programs for mothers, nutrition, and medical care. To learn more about MPI, contact www. mpi-inc.org.

To make a donation of $10 or more or to order *God Guides* books for $5 plus postage, contact

Lynn Gann at:

MPI

PO Box 8445

Holland, MI 49422

A More Excellent Gift

My friend, Karen Mulder's husband, Larry, founder of ODL, a door light manufacturing company in Zeeland, Michigan, sent this note to his employees a few years ago:

Perhaps, if you are an employer, this is just the kind of gift you would like to give your employees or even to a friend.

As long as I can remember I have purchased
some small Christmas gift for you.
When Karen and I were looking for
this year's "just- the-right-thing" gift,
we found out about the Alternative Christmas Market.

When I discovered, for example, that eye surgery could
save someone's sight in Ghana for $16, it caused me to
think "Holy Smoke! What a Christmas gift to give someone!"

So, I thought that maybe you'd like to give this type
of present to someone in the world and I'd like to pay
for it as my present to you.

The enclosed shopping list gives a number of options.
Pick any combination up to $16 total and print your
name at the bottom. Put it in one of the boxes on the
table in my office by Friday night (December 9).

I'll see to it that all of the gifts are sent to the proper place.

I hope this pleases you as much as a candle or candy!

Merry Christmas and thank you.

Larry

Gifts that Make a Difference

Angel Tree

Angel tree was started by Ms. Beard for prisoners to be able to give gifts to their children at Christmastime. Paper angels can be found hanging from trees in malls. Choose a paper angel and shop for that child whose name appears on the card. www.angeltree.org or call 800-552-6435.

Make-A-Wish Foundation

Why not turn gift-giving into wish giving this holiday season? The Make-A-Wish Foundation grants the wishes of kids with life-threatening illness. Call 800-772-WISH or visit www.wish.org. Go to: "Supporters", then "Promotions to Give Back".

Gifts for Art Enthusiasts

Do you have an art enthusiast on your list? Shopping for gifts from the world's great museums and cultural attractions doesn't even require a plane ticket. MuseumShop.com brings together over 3,500 treasures (priced from $10-$6,000) from institutions as exotic as the Louvre and as down-home as the Minneapolis Institute of Art. A portion of every purchase directly supports the programs of that museum. To order, call 888-872-0080 or go online to www.museumshop.com and 'visit' international museums while you shop.

Gifts for Animal Lovers

If you have animal lovers on your gift list, here are some ideas they'll be wild about. There's a whole kingdom of selections. For less than $15, you can pick a stuffed animal — kangaroo, tiger, bear or wolf. Thanks to a partnership between the World Wildlife Federation and the Discovery

Channel/Nature Company store, a portion of the purchase price will go to help to protect endangered animal habitats. To choose your adoptee at Discovery Channel/Nature Company stores nationwide, call 877-DCI-STORE or visit: www.discoverystore.com.

Mama and Baby Bears

Do you know someone who could use a bear hug? For the kid or kid-at-heart, the Susan Bear or Susan Mini Bear would delight a child's heart. Cute and Cuddly, both Mama (14", $20) and Baby (6", $6) are just right for kids aged four and older. The Susan G. Koeman Breast Cancer Foundation also offers supportive stocking stuffers including Milestones to Wellness — a collection of 13 marble refrigerator magnets for $15 — and Race for the Cure pink ribbon socks ($6/pair). Call 877-SGK-SHOP or visit www.breastcancerinfo.com.

Adopt an Animal

In addition to gift memberships, many zoos offer their own adoption programs that provide a host of perks for the "foster parents". Zoo gift shops are likely to stock a variety of animal-friendly presents too. Visit store.fonz.org for the National Zoo in Washington D.C. or www.shopzoo.com for the San Diego zoo.

Growing Gifts

Tree Planting Gift

Looking for something to give a friend or an entire family? The National Arbor Day Foundation, a nonprofit organization committed to helping people plant and care for trees, offers a Trees In Celebration which will put a smile on the receiver's face. To honor your friend or family, for each $10 donation made, 10 trees will be planted in natural forests that have been destroyed. Recipients will receive a certificate with proof. To place an order, call 888-448-7337 or visit www.arborday.org.

Gardening Gift

Start a plant from one of your house or garden plants. Include a note indicating that the plant has been rooted from your (name variety) plant and that it represents a life rooted in Christ's love or that Christ was born from the "root of Jesse", king David's father. (Isaiah 11:1).

A container planted with a variety of herbs becomes a welcomed gift. You might want to include a few herb recipes or the beautiful cookbook, Recipes from a French Herb Garden by Geraldene Holt or Michigan Herb Cookbook by Suzanne Breckenridge and Marjorie Snyder.

A one-year gift membership to the American Horticultural Society is just right for the expert or novice gardener on your list. One of the oldest nonprofit gardening organizations, the AHS educates people on becoming environmentally responsible, and works to advance the art and science of horticulture. For your $35 gift donation your friend will receive the twice-monthly publication the American Gardener, a toll-free number offering gardening information services, free seed-exchange program with other members and reduced and free admissions to public gardens and flower shows nationwide. Call 800-777-7931 or visit www.ahs.org.

A growing plant with instructions for care makes a welcomed gift.

Gifts for the Health Nut (Or Those You Encourage To Be)

Gifts for those with good intentions for bettering their physical well-being in the coming year might include:

- Trip to a spa (Canyon Ranch in Tucson, Arizona or Lenox, Massachusetts is an excellent choice)
- Health Club Membership
- Yoga/Pilates sessions
- Ingredients for a healthy meal and the recipe
- Healthy food cookbook: *Greens: A Country Garden Cookbook* by Stella Kraus; *The Gluten-Free Bible*, for those for whom "the staff of life" is slow poison, *Eat Yourself Beautiful* by Daniele de Winter; *Pure Vegetarian* by Charlie Trotter; or *I Can't Believe this Has No Sugar* by Deborah E. Buhr
- Workout clothes (Lulu Lemon is a preferred brand.)
- Exercise equipment

Monetary Gifts Uniquely Given

Nancy Doeden has a unique way to give monetary gifts to her grandchildren. She gives each of them a verse, written on a 3X5 card. (For example: Luke 1:30, "But the angel said to her, Do not be afraid, Mary, you have found favor with God. You will be with child and give birth to a son, and you are to give him the name Jesus".) The child then looks for something in the house that relates to the clue in the verse. In this case the money is hidden under the crèche statue of Mary. Other clues in different verses relate to objects in the house under which the money is hidden.

Personalized Name Photos

Nancy also gives personalized gifts to friends and family members. She takes photos of architectural aspects on buildings and from signs which incorporate letters, arranging them to spell the person's name

She then has individual pieces of glass cut for each photo and arranges for a framing store to attach metal holders to connect the glass pieces. The individual photos are then arranged to spell a person's name. Alternatively, have the framing store attach the photos to heavy cork backing. Include a wooden tray in order to display the tiles.

Gifts of the Spirit

Gift of Blessing

The prophet Simeon offered blessings to the baby Jesus and his parents (Luke 2:25-35). Your blessings too can greatly influence the lives of others when shared in these fun-to-give ways:

- Write a love letter to your child or significant other.
- Frame your child's or friend's name and its meaning.
- Give a memory to your parents by recording or writing about a shared event that was most meaningful to you.

Gift of Support

Like Aaron and Hur upholding the hands of Moses (Exodus 17:10-13), offer your friendship and support to someone who may be alone this Christmas.

- Take a picnic lunch to share with a shut-in or nursing-home resident.

- Send a note or email to an out-of-town friend struggling with a difficult problem. Assure them of your prayers for them.
- Invite a single parent and child to join your family during the holiday.

Gift of a Meaningful Luncheon Experience

My gift to my friends each year is a Christmas luncheon given the first Saturday of December. I choose a theme at the beginning of each year. Then I watch for key verses surrounding the theme and for a story to read throughout the year, etc.

I send invitations to my guests four weeks before the event.

Each participant is asked to share something at the luncheon in connection with the theme. We enjoy appetizers and socialize for an hour.

Once we are seated at the table (I have name cards at each place), I share a meditation on the theme, a poem or thought about friendship, an appropriate story and then a prayer. As we are eating lunch each woman has a chance to share her thoughts on the theme.

Everyone leaves with a meaningful book or favor that will help her to remember the day and the theme.

The event makes for a very warm and meaningful time of friendship and also prepares everyone to hopefully gain a proper perspective on Advent at the outset.

I always pray for the Holy Spirit to give me a theme. Those that I have used are:

Stars
Angels
Mary
Joseph
Wise men
Shepherds

God's Surprising Presence
Waiting
Joy
Peace
Light
Hope
Holiness
Journey to Bethlehem
Watching for God
Preparing for the Christ of Christmas
God's Kingdom
God's Grace
God's Majesty
Gratitude

Sample Luncheon Agenda

1.Welcome/purpose of luncheon: to celebrate friendships and to honor Jesus, whose birth we celebrate

2. Tribute to friendship – (example):

"In an evening class at Stanford University, the last lecture was on the mind-body connection – the relationship between stress and disease. The speaker (head of Psychiatry at Stanford) said, among other things, that one of the best things a man could do for his health is to be married to a woman, whereas for a woman, one of the best things she could do for her health was to nurture her relationships with her girlfriends. At first everyone laughed, but he was serious.

Women connect with each other differently and provide support systems that help each other to deal with stress and difficult life experiences. Physically, this quality "girlfriend time" helps us to create more serotonin – a neurotransmitter that helps combat depression and can create a general feeling of well-being.

Women share feelings, whereas men often form relationships around activities. We share from our souls, and evidently that is very GOOD for our health.

He said that spending time with a friend is just as important to our general health as jogging or working out at a gym.

There's a tendency to think that when we are "exercising" we are doing something good for our bodies, but when we are hanging out with friends, we are wasting our time and should be more productively engaged – not true. In fact, he said that failure to create and maintain quality personal relationships with other humans is as dangerous to our physical health as smoking!

So every time you hang out to schmooze with a gal pal, just pat yourself on the back and congratulate yourself for doing something good for your health! We are indeed very, very fortunate! So let's toast to our friendship with our girlfriends. Evidently it's very good for our health!"

3. Sharing of a story or Biblical history – The following is a message that I shared at a luncheon during which I used the theme "Waiting".

Theme – Waiting

As I have studied the history of the patriarchs, those founding fathers of Judaism, I was struck by a theme which emerged for me.

Sarai **waited** for the long-promised child that would be the predecessor of the Jewish race. From, him, God promised, his offspring would be more than the stars of the sky. How could this be? Could an old lady bear a child? It seemed ludicrous! Yet God appeared to Abram fourteen years later and reaffirmed his promise. "At this time next year Sarai will bear a son, and you will call him Isaac."

And sure enough, the promise came true. Sarai bore a son named Isaac at age ninety-nine! Hadn't God said, "Is anything too hard for the Lord?" (Genesis 18:14)

God changed Abram's name to Abraham and Sarai's name to Sarah, thereby exchanging names and giving them an H sound from His name, *Yahweh*. God took their names, calling himself *The God of Abraham, Isaac and Jacob.* (In the New Testament/Covenant we are called *Christ*ians and Jesus is called *The Son of Man.*) This was an integral part of the ritual of covenant-making in those times.

David, king of the Jews, was born of Jesse through Jacob's son, Judah. He was born and lived in Bethlehem and the prophet, Micah prophesied that Jesus would be born in Bethlehem, city of King David. (Likewise, many other prophecies pointed to Jesus as the promised Messiah – 456 in all.)

Sure enough! 2000 years after God made the covenant with Abraham and 700 years after Micah's prophecy, the Christ child was born of Mary in Bethlehem, the city of her and Joseph's ancestors! The time of waiting was over. The long-awaited Messiah had finally come to earth to redeem mankind from his sins and restore a broken world to wholeness and oneness with God.

James Stewart wrote, "So the Redeemer came. Somewhere in the mind and the heart of God from the foundation of the earth, the Christ had been waiting, hidden in the counsels of eternity until the great bell of the ages should strike; and when at last everything in the world and in the souls of men was ready and prepared, He came, the Word of God, made flesh, not a moment early and not a moment late, but exactly on the stroke of the hour. It was the "Day of the Lord."

Waiting can be agonizing and often we wonder why God is slow to answer our prayers but if we truly trust God, we are assured that His timing is perfect and is a part of His amazing plan for all creation.

God's plan was to bring Jesus to earth at the perfect time – when the Roman roads were constructed, when there was a universal language and when Israel was the crossroads of the world, enabling the gospel message to travel quickly to all known countries.

4. Old Testament reading:

On this mountain (Zion) the Lord of hosts
will make for all peoples
a feast of rich food, a feast of well-aged wines...
Then the Lord God will wipe away the tears from all faces,
and the disgrace of his people
he will take away from all the earth,
for the Lord has spoken.
It will be said on that day,
lo, this is our God; we have
waited *for him, so that he might save us.*
*This is the Lord for whom we have **waited**;*
let us be glad and rejoice in his salvation.
Isaiah 25:6, 8-9

5. New Testament fulfillment:

So Joseph also (along with the others who were from the
lineage of King David) went up from the town of Nazareth
in Galilee to Judea, to Bethlehem the town of David,
because he belonged to the house and line of David. He
went there to register with Mary, who was pledged to be
married to him and was expecting a child. While they were
there, the time came for the baby to be born, and she gave
birth to her firstborn, a son. She wrapped him in cloths
and placed him in a manger, because there was no room
for them in the inn.

Luke 2:4-7(NIV)

Passionate Waiting

If it is true that God in Jesus Christ is waiting for our response to divine love, then we can discover a whole new perspective on how to wait in life. We can learn to be obedient people who do not always try to go back to the action but who recognize the fulfillment of our deepest humanity in passion, in waiting. If we can do this, I am convinced that we will come in touch with the glory of God and our own new life.[1]

Henri J.M. Nouwen

6. Challenge

Present a challenge for the season. Example:

I encourage you, during this Advent season, to be especially mindful of being kind and appreciative of service persons (store clerks, waiters, etc). Look them in the eye, remember their names, compliment them on a job well done, and wish them a blessed Christmas (*not* Happy Holidays!) Tip them well. Your kindness may be the only moment of true caring that they experience in the midst of a difficult day.

7. Prayer

Dear God, these are my friends whom I love and cherish. Help them to live their lives to the fullest. Encourage them to excel beyond their expectations. Allow them to shine in the darkest places where loving is most difficult and yet of immense need. Protect them with your angels at all times. Lift them up when their need for you is greatest. Grant them the awareness that, as they walk with You, they walk in the safety of Your limitless care. May this be a Christmas season in which they are acutely aware of your great love which led to Your giving the ultimate gift of all time, that of the Savior of all mankind. Inspire our hearts through the sharing of our thoughts. Amen.

Be pleased to be our guest at this table as we enjoy sumptuous food and rich fellowship with one another. Amen.

8. Allow guests to share musings on the topic.

While lunch is being served you might want to give your guests an opportunity to share something that they have been waiting for or had waited for in the past. (I always include a "heads up" on the topic in the invitation). My experience has been that this time of sharing is a very warm and memorable part of the luncheon.

Take Home Gift

As a take home favor I gave an inexpensive antique silver spoon (silver plated spoons cost $1- $10) to each guest tied with a ribbon holding the verse, Genesis 18:14, "Is there anything too hard for the Lord?" I explained to them that, because Isaac was a child of promise, the one through whom the Messiah would come, he, of all persons was born with "a silver spoon in his mouth!" An alternative gift could be Ben Patterson's excellent book, *Waiting*.

A meaningful luncheon experience – preparing friends for Advent
Left to right: Karen Mulder, B.J Visscher, Jean Smith, Jan Kramer,
Nelda Briggs, Ginger Jurries, Linda George, Meena Ariagno, Cathy
Bouws, Tami Elhart, Ruth Beckman, Helen Komejan, Annie Mitchell

Compile a Recipe Booklet

One Christmas I compiled a booklet of tasty, nutritious recipes and gave it to friends who I thought would appreciate a cookbook.

How to compile a cookbook:

- Select favorite recipes.
- Type them on your computer/transfer to a flash drive.
- Design an attractive cover.
- Have copies printed and spiral-bound at a printing company.
- Distribute to delighted recipients with a Christmas wish for delicious times of dining together and enjoying one another's fellowship.

Gourmet Greats
a potpourri of nutritious gastronomical creations

by Ginger Jurries

A compilation of favorite recipes makes a special and useful personal gift.

Adopt-a-Family

One woman in California shared a wonderful project that her family discovered. She explained that for several years her family contacted a nonprofit organization called the Box Project. Founded in 1962 by Mrs. Martin Luther King Jr., this organization matches families nationwide with needy families in the south.

The California family then "adopted" a family in rural Mississippi that was living below the poverty level, sending it much-needed help and gifts. The California mother commented that the relationship her family developed with the Mississippi family blossomed, and now they help their adopted family year-round. For example, when they realized there weren't any Christmas gifts their adopted family really needed or wanted, they decided to pay the family's utility bill.

For details on this project, send a self-addressed stamped envelope to Box Project, P.O. Box 435, Plainville, CT 06062.

Low-Budget Gifts

Who wouldn't enjoy receiving these low-cost gifts?

CD's: Share your favorite Christmas carols and sacred music with a customized CD. Design your personal list of favorites and download them onto a disc from a legal online music service. Using a CD-packaging kit (available at office supply stores), create a label by scanning cheerful wrapping paper or use clip art or photographs. Print the design on the label that comes with the kit. On card stock, print a playlist with "liner notes," personal anecdotes related to the songs. Package each with a disc in a heavy, square envelope.

Yummy, Affordable Gifts

Include a recipe with a favorite food item. The following are sure to be welcomed gifts:

Cajun Cocktail Nuts

½ cup (1 stick) butter melted
2 Tbl. worcestershire sauce
2 tsp. chili powder
1 pound unsalted cashews
1 pound raw pecans
1 pound raw almonds
Garlic salt

Preheat oven to 275 degrees.

Mix butter and worcestershire sauce in large roasting pan and drizzle with butter mixture, stirring to coat. Bake 45 minutes, stirring every 15 minutes. Spread on paper towels to dry.

Season with garlic salt and black pepper. Wrap in clear, cellophane paper bags tied with a bright holiday ribbon.

Three Types of Vinaigrette

Ginger-Basil Vinaigrette

Use this sauce for fish or shrimp, crisp lettuce, avocado, or rice.

Process ½ cup loosely packed **fresh basil leaves**, chopped; 1 tsp. **grated fresh ginger**, juice squeezed out; 1 **garlic clove**, minced; 1 tsp. **honey**; and a few grinds **sea salt** in a food processor until smooth. With processor running, pour 2/3 cup olive or grapeseed oil through food chute in a slow, steady stream, processing until smooth. Makes about ¾ cup.

Peach-Poppy Seed Vinaigrette

Pair with any lettuce, or drizzle over grilled pork.

Process ¾ cup fresh or frozen sliced **peaches or mango**, thawed; 3 T. **peach preserves**; 2T plus 2 tsp. **apple cider vinegar**; ½ tsp. **Dijon mustard**; and ½ t. **sea salt** in a food processor until smooth. With processor running, pour ½ cup **canola or olive oil** through food chute in a slow stream. Process until smooth; stir in 1 ½ tsp. **poppy seeds**. Makes 1¼ cups.

Red Pepper Jelly Vinaigrette

Pair this sweet, piquant vinaigrette with fresh greens and tangy goat cheese. It also works as a marinade for chicken or pork.

Whisk together 6 T. **red wine vinegar**; 3 T. red **pepper jelly**; 1 **shallot**, minced (about 2 T.); 1 T. **coarse-grained mustard**; ¼ t. **sea salt**; and ¼ t. **black pepper** in a small bowl. Pour olive 1/3 cup **olive oil** through food chute in a slow stream. Makes about 1 cup.

Package these dressings in attractive bottles, available at your local grocery or kitchen store.

Chocolate Zucchini Cakes

2 cups sugar
½ cup butter, softened
½ cup canola oil
3 large eggs
2 1/3 cups all-purpose flour
2/3 cup unsweetened cocoa
1 tsp. baking soda
1 tsp. table salt
½ tsp. ground cinnamon
2/3 cup whole buttermilk

2 cups grated unpeeled zucchini (about 2 medium)
1 (4-0z.) semisweet chocolate baking bar, finely chopped
2 tsp. vanilla extract
6 (5X3 inch) disposable aluminum foil loaf pans, lightly
    greased

1. Preheat oven to 350 degrees. Beat first three ingredients at medium speed with a heavy-duty electric stand mixer until light and fluffy. Add eggs, 1 at a time, beating just until blended after each addition. Sift together flour and next four ingredients; add to the butter mixture alternately with buttermilk, beginning and ending with the flour mixture. Beat at low speed just until blended. Stir zucchini and next two ingredients into batter until blended. Spoon batter into lightly greased loaf pans, filling 2/3 full. For neat travel, bake in paper bakeware, Go to welcomehomebrands.com.

2. Bake for 30-35 minutes or until a wooden pick inserted in the center comes out clean. Cool completely in pans on wire racks (about an hour). Leave in pans.

3. Prepare Chocolate Fudge Frosting. Spoon hot frosting over cooled cakes (about ¼ cup each); cool completely (about 30 minutes). Package in cellophane bags. Tie with an attractive, colorful ribbon.

Chocolate Fudge Frosting

1/3 cup butter
1/3 cup unsweetened cocoa
1/3 cup milk
¼ cup sour cream
2 tsp. vanilla extract
3 cups powdered sugar

Cook first three ingredients in a large saucepan over medium heat, stirring constantly, three to four minutes or until butter melts. Remove from heat; whisk in sour cream and vanilla until blended. Gradually add powdered sugar, beating at medium speed with an electric mixer until smooth. Enjoy!

See also *The Heart of Christmas* by Hearst Books or *What Should I Bring? Great Gifts for Every Occasion* by Alison Boteler for more ideas for food gift ideas. You will find some delicious gifts to make on Donna Sawyer's website: donnasawyerwow.com.

CHAPTER 9

CHRISTMAS TRIVIA

The Story Behind the Song, "I Heard the Bells on Christmas Day"

During a Christmas cantata last year, I listened to the words of this piercing song for the first time, *I Heard the Bells on Christmas Day*. The cynical tone in the third verse amazed me.

Why so bleak for a joyous season?

Henry Wadsworth Longfellow's journals tell the story. In 1863, when the poet penned the poem, originally called "Christmas Bells," peace on earth was only a dream. The Civil War had torn most every American family with horror and despair.

Longfellow's family was not an exception. The day the poet heard the Christmas bells, he also received the heart-wrenching news that his son, a lieutenant in the Army of the Potomac, had been seriously wounded in battle. As the bells chimed "peace on earth, peace on earth," his son was dying, the result of man's hate. Longfellow struggled with the conflicting messages.

"There is not peace on earth," he wrote. "Hate is strong/And peals the song/Of peace on earth/Good will to men."

But the bells kept ringing and ringing. It was as if God, who also lost a Son to man's vengeance, said: Hate is strong, but I am stronger. Rest in Me, peace will come.[1]

The Story behind the Song, "O little Town of Bethlehem"

Phillips Brooks, a Boston bachelor and Philadelphia preacher, wrote the words for this hymn in 1868 as a poem for children. While teaching Sunday school after the horrors of the Civil War, Brooks longed to impart the peace he had experienced on a journey through the Holy Land. In 1865 he had ridden on horseback from Jerusalem to Bethlehem and nearby fields — the resting place of shepherds who watched their flocks by night. That evening, he attended a worship service at the Ancient Church of the Nativity, built by Constantine in 326 on the site that tradition says is where Jesus was born. Brooks marveled at how God could come to earth in such a quiet, lowly way. But how, he wondered, could he pass on this awe to others?

A poem didn't seem like enough. Brooks asked Lewis Redner, the church organist, to set his words to music so the children could sing it for a Christmas service. But Redner struggled to find a fitting tune. The night before the service there was still no melody.

Weary and discouraged, Redner went to bed. He felt he had disappointed his friend, the children, himself and God.

Sometime in the night a sweet, angelic melody broke through his fog of sleep. God was speaking. Redner sprang from bed to jot down the notes, fitting them to Brooks' words until dawn: "Our hopes and fears of all the years will rest in Thee tonight."

Christmas morning, he taught the thirty six children and six teachers the new song. The hymn became so popular that when Brooks, who never married or had children of his own, died at age 58, the nation mourned. But one of his five-year-old friends, a devoted Sunday school student, said knowingly, "Oh Mother, how happy the angels will be!"[2]

The History of the Candy Cane

A candy maker in Indiana wanted to make a candy that would be a testimony of the true meaning of Christmas. So he invented the Christmas Candy Cane. The candy man incorporated several symbols for the birth, ministry, and death of Jesus Christ. He began with a stick of pure white hard candy: "white" to symbolize the Virgin Birth and the sinless nature of Jesus, and "hard" to symbolize the Solid Rock, the foundation of the Church, and firmness of the promises of God.

The candy maker made the candy in the form of a "J" to represent the precious name of Jesus, who came to earth as our Savior. It could also represent the staff of the "Good Shepherd" with which He reaches down into the ditches of the world to lift out the fallen lambs who, like all sheep, have gone astray.

Thinking that the candy was somewhat plain, the candy maker stained it with red stripes. He used small stripes to show the stripes of the scourging Jesus received by which we are "healed" from our sin. The large red stripe was for the blood which was shed by Christ on the cross so that we could have the promise of eternal life.

This Christmas symbol, the candy cane, can remind you of the true meaning of Christmas as you celebrate this year.[3]

Candy canes have a special purpose in the history of the church.

The Origin of the Crèche

The créche (literally "crib") is believed to have its origins with St. Francis of Assisi. He was concerned because the people seemed not to understand what Christ's birth was like or fully appreciate the events surrounding his birth in a barn with animals in attendance; how the shepherds on the hillside were surprised by the angels or how the Three Kings came from far away to pay homage to the Babe.

In 1223 Francis created the first known crèche — a real-life reenactment of Christ's birth — at the church in Greccio, near Assisi, Italy. At first he included a newborn baby in a manger and Mary and Joseph. In the following years he added the other participants in the nativity story. On Christmas Eve people came from nearby villages to see the scene. This popular custom quickly spread throughout Europe.

If we remember St. Francis' concern that the people be able to see graphically what the first nativity was like, then we will look on our own crèche differently. While there are beautiful and expensive sets to be had, there is also a special meaning when a child's favorite dolls or play figures are used to tell the Christmas story. This reminds him that God chose ordinary people and commonplace events to attend the miraculous birth of Christ. The old and chipped plaster figurines from our own childhood, which we faithfully display year after year, undermine the rich tradition and meaning of Christmas. Time spent painting greenware, carving figures, or building our own stable, provides opportunity for quiet reflection as we create with our own hands symbols that, for years to come, will remind us of God's wonderful gift.[4]

The Significance of the Color Purple

You may have noticed that during the Advent season, some churches display the color purple in their sanctuaries, and some display the color blue. And you may have even heard that the color purple is the color of royalty, but do you know why? Well, it all has to do with expensive snails!

Thousands of years ago, when Christ was living on the earth, the color purple was the most expensive dye to produce — only kings could afford such fashionable extravagance. In fact, one ounce of dye (the weight of just five nickels and one penny) cost much more than an entire pound of gold. Why was it so expensive? Believe it or not, the royal dye, called *tekhelet* in Hebrew, was squeezed from snails — a type of mollusk! The extracts were boiled down and mixed with other chemicals to make just the right color. It would take over 10,000 mollusks to make enough dye for just one toga or robe. The process was lost somewhere in the eighth century AD and people throughout history have spent years trying to recreate the dye because of the mystery over whether it was purple or blue.

In ancient documents, the color *tekhelet* is often described as violet, but other sources refer to it as the same color as the sky or sea, which would mean it was blue. Even today, scientists are analyzing biological, chemical and archaeological data to try and figure it out, but no one has been able to find an answer. Regardless of whether your church chooses to use purple or blue in the weeks leading up to Christmas, the meaning is the same. During Advent we prepare the way and honor Christ the Lord, the one true King, with the most royal color we can find.[5]

The Meaning of the Star of Bethlehem

The star is a very significant symbol of Christmas. We know that there was a bright star that led the wise men to the place where Jesus was living. The star takes on greater meaning, however, when we know the way in which it was conjoined to produce an exceptionally brilliant light.

In the year that Christ was born (6 BC) there was a conjunction of planets: **Jupiter**, the king planet (so named because it is so huge that it takes twelve years to rotate around the sun) formed a figure 8 with **Venus**, the mother planet in the constellation known as The Sign of the Fishes. It was the brightest star anyone had ever seen or will ever see! Jupiter was styled the "King's Planet" because it represented the highest King and ruler of the universe. The Sign of the Fishes meant that a divine and cosmic ruler was to appear in Palestine at a culmination of history. This may help to explain why the Magi were well enough informed to look for a "King of the Jews" in Palestine. Today we use the fish symbol to designate that we are Christians because of this astrological association.

Paul Maier writes that this Biblical verse need not imply any sudden visible movements on the part of the astral phenomenon. Because of the rotation of the earth, anything in the night sky appears to move westward as the night progresses, except Polaris and the relatively few stars north of it. And as people travel, the stars do seem to move with them or before them, stopping when they stop. So when it reached a zenith in the skies over Bethlehem, the gleaming blue-white star of Christmas would indeed have seemed to stop for the Magi as they reached their destination.

The Magi (many more than just three) traveled from Mesopotamia, Persia (now known as Iran) or Babylon (now known as Iraq.) These priest-sages, extremely well educated for their day, were specialists in medicine, religion, astronomy, astrology, divination and magic, and their caste eventually spread across much of the east. As in any other profession, there were both good and bad magi, depending on whether they did research in the sciences or practiced augury, necromancy, and magic. The Persian magi were credited with higher religious and intellectual attainments, while the Babylonian magi were sometimes deemed imposters.

Whatever the origin of the eastern sages, their visit was of great significance for later Christianity; the Wise Men were pagans, not Hebrews, and the fact that Gentile magi performed the same adoration as Jewish shepherds symbolized the universal outreach for future Christianity. "Nations (*Gentiles*) shall come to your light", the prophet Isaiah had written, "and kings to the brightness of your dawn." (Isaiah 60:3)

The prediction about Jesus being born in Bethlehem came from the Old Testament: "But you, Bethlehem, Ephrathah, though you are small among the clans of Judah, out of you will come for me one who will be ruler over Israel, whose origins are from of old, from ancient times." (Micah 5:2)

Perhaps the wise men had read that prophecy and were so eager to see the King, (who by then was a toddler,) that they traveled approximately 700 miles by camel, partly through the desert, to see Him!

Matthew records that these men were overjoyed when they saw the star. Can't you image their jubilation as they finally witnessed this once-in-a lifetime event — beholding this child-King whose birth had been predicted for approximately 700 years! "The star went before the magi until it stopped over the place where the child was." (Matthew 2:9)

Take time to conclude this study on the myriad ways to creatively celebrate Advent with a prayer of thanks to our Savior, Jesus the Christ. Thank Him for the greatest gift ever given, that of salvation and abundant life offered to all who will accept it.

Christmas Continues

When the flurry of gifting is stilled,
When the guests have all gone home,
When the decorations are well tucked away,
When the pageants have had their day,
The work of Christmas begins:
To find the lost,
To heal the hurting,
To feed the hungry,
To encourage the downtrodden,
To invite the stranger,
To bring peace to our families,
To join our hearts in worship and song.
Ginger Jurries

Boxed Memories

Disrobing the Christmas tree
Seems strikingly symbolic
Of tucking, in memory boxes,
Declarations of the year just past.
Shining gold balls represent
Approving plaudits of my noblest accomplishments.
Each stalwart angel reminds me of a time
That God, in his grace, protected me from harm.
Little glass bells seem to ring
In thanks for the wealth of blessings I've received.
And the garland of lights marks the succession of spent days,
Spiraling upward to the star,
Pinpointing the Wonder of Christmas,
Jesus, the center of my totality.
Ginger Jurries

CHAPTER 10

CELEBRATE EPIPHANY

Epiphany means *to show forth* or *to manifest*. It is the church year which extends from January 6 through Ash Wednesday. It commemorates the revealing of Jesus as the Christ (Savior) to the Gentiles by the Magi (wise men.)

Many churches celebrate this event every January 6. The following are some ways to observe Epiphany at home:

- Remove all the ornaments from your Christmas tree, leaving only the lights. This will probably only work if your tree is artificial since a live tree will no longer be fresh. Alternately, you could hang Christmas lights from the mantle or draperies.
- Bake a Bundt cake. (See page 30 for recipe.) Frost it and put gumdrops on the top to form a circle that resembles a king's (wise men's) crown. Insert foil-wrapped dimes or quarters to symbolize the gifts of gold given to Jesus. Whoever gets a piece of the cake containing a coin gets to keep it.
- Have a ceremony in front of the tree. Turn off the lights except for those on the tree and a small light for reading. Select verses from the Bible to read aloud relating to light. The following are possibilities:

    Isaiah 2:5
    Isaiah 42:6

Isaiah 49:6
Acts 13:47
Matthew 5:14-16
John 1:1-5
Philippians 2:14-16

- Read the story of the coming of the wise men to Jesus when he was a toddler from Matthew 2:1-12. Discuss how the wise men must have felt as they approached their final destination and how they reacted to the bright star. Also talk about what Mary and Joseph's reaction might have been to these exotic visitors.
- Read some ideas on being a light from the book, *Be an Angel* by Dana Reynolds.
- Tell what you have done to be a light to others in the coming year. Record your ideas.
- Dress in king's costumes (make crowns from poster board or don ones from a fast food restaurant and use bed sheets or towels for the king's cape.)
- Hide notes in each child's room containing validations of things you appreciate and admire about him or her. Just as the wise men searched for Jesus, tell each child that he or she will also embark on a search for something of value. Be sure to save their validations for each child in a notebook or treasure box to read at other times of the year. These can be updated and expanded for birthdays or other times of the year.
- Just as the wise men left treasure for Joseph, Mary and Jesus, so Patrick Connolly, a well-respected Seattle newsman at the Associated Press, left valuable treasure for his children. Patrick shared his love, values and talents with his boys through notes, cartoons and humor. Connolly compiled hundreds of these treasures into a book for his children called, *Love, Dad*. An untimely heart attack at age 42 took Connolly from his family, but they had the wonderful legacy by which to remember him.

Perhaps Patrick's idea of leaving a written treasure is so
you would like to do for your children.
- Read the following rule or better yet, write it in script on your
computer, print and frame it. Hang it in a prominent place in
your home.

> Do all the good you can,
> By all the means you can,
> In all the places you can,
> At all the times you can,
> To all the people you can,
> As long as you can.[1]
>> John Wesley

CHAPTER 11

HOLIDAY EVENTS DIARY

An Advent diary is an excellent way to record your reflections, hopes, and prayers during the Advent season. Keeping it active from year to year will provide an excellent history of your cherished Christmas memories.

A few suggestions:

- Invite each family member to make entries. Young children can verbally dictate their memories for an adult to record. Encourage your child to include his or her Christmas prayers, perhaps even a letter to Jesus.
- Illustrate your diary with cutouts from favorite Christmas cards. Include mementos of the holiday season in your Advent diary — a program from a special event, a photograph or sketch of a winter scene or your family in front of the tree.
- Enter the activities that worked well for your family as well as those that bombed. Some activities will obviously be more suited to younger children and some to older ones.
- Enter in your diary a copy of the things your children/ grandchildren made for others, programs in which they participated with a photo of them as well the most memorable events of the Christmas season.

Keep your diary personal. Let this be a place where you express yourself in a private, intimate way. Use your diary as a means of recording:

- your insights into the Christmas story and the Advent season
- your spiritual longings and desires
- your hopes and expectations for what Christ will accomplish in and through your life in the coming year
- your reflections on the symbols of the season

Keep your diary Christ-centered.

You may find yourself feeling at odds with the materialism and commercialism around you. You may be feeling lonely or disappointed at dreams and hopes unfulfilled, or perhaps you are feeling a little sad as you experience long winter nights and short, colder days. Perhaps the festivities clash with feelings of loneliness over the loss of a loved one. Express your thoughts in terms of what Christ means to you in that feeling. What does it mean for Jesus to arrive in the crowded bustle of your overstuffed holiday agenda? How will you make adjustments to accomplish a more Christ-centered, peace-filled Advent season next year? Your entries in your diary need not be long; they may be only a few words. They need not be world-class prose or poetry; they need only be genuine expressions from your heart. Advent is a time for letting your heart feel the heartbeat of the Lord.

Year_____

Events

_____
_____
_____
_____
_____
_____
_____
_____
_____
_____
_____
_____
_____
_____

Acts of Kindness

_____
_____
_____
_____
_____
_____
_____
_____
_____
_____
_____
_____
_____
_____

Programs, Photos, etc.

Year_____

Events

_____
_____
_____
_____
_____
_____
_____
_____
_____
_____
_____
_____
_____
_____

Acts of Kindness

_____
_____
_____
_____
_____
_____
_____
_____
_____
_____
_____
_____
_____

Programs, Photos, etc.

Year_____

Events

_____
_____
_____
_____
_____
_____
_____
_____
_____
_____
_____
_____
_____
_____
_____

Acts of Kindness

_____
_____
_____
_____
_____
_____
_____
_____
_____
_____
_____
_____
_____
_____
_____

Programs, Photos, etc.

Year_____

Events

_____
_____
_____
_____
_____
_____
_____
_____
_____
_____
_____
_____
_____
_____
_____

Acts of Kindness

_____
_____
_____
_____
_____
_____
_____
_____
_____
_____
_____
_____
_____
_____

Programs, Photos, etc.

CHAPTER 12

RESOURCES THAT MAKE MEMORIES

Books

Chicken Soup for the Soul, The Gift of Christmas

Jack Canfield, Mark Victor Hansen & Amy Newmark
A special collection of joyful Holiday stories

First Christmas

Paul L. Maier
Harper & Row, Publishers
This insightful classic combines history, geography and archaeology to provide fascinating facts that verify the Biblical story of Christ's coming to earth.

Have Yourself a Stressless Little Christmas

Darla Satterfield Davis
Whitestone Books
Toss those mile-long holiday "To Do" lists in the garbage and transform your holiday with this priceless, tiny treasure—packed full of guilt-free short cuts and energy saving tips.

How the Grinch Stole Christmas

Dr. Seuss
Random House
Told in whimsical rhyme, Dr. Seuss style, this delightful book makes a significant point in regard to Christmas celebrations. A despicable protagonist, namely The Grinch, conspires with his faithful dog, Max, to steal Christmas from the Whos down in Whoville. He, however, makes an amazing discovery on Christmas morning which forces him to conclude that, "Maybe Christmas doesn't come from a store, maybe Christmas is a little bit more!"

Hundred Dollar Holiday

Bill Mc Kibben
Published by Simon & Schuster 1998
McKibben not only gives many great ideas for making Christmas meaningful but this attractive 8X 4" book is a little treasure to give to relatives (along with the one you are holding) to encourage others to adopt some of your ideas for reclaiming Christmas. Peace will come when you find that Christmas can't be store bought. No longer will you dread the holiday season. The hustle and bustle will be eliminated, and silently God will impart the blessings of His heaven.

Mary Did You Know?

Mark Lowry
Published by Waterbrook Press
Many of us have heard this hauntingly beautiful song by Mark Lowry, but now we can get inspired by the beautiful illustrations and child-like text. This is sure to become a family favorite.

Preparing for Jesus

Walter Wangerin Jr.
Published by Zondervan Publishing House
Wangerin gives us an inspiring devotional that affords the reader a new perspective on the meaning of Christmas. It beautifully prepares the reader's heart for the arrival of the baby Jesus.

St. Nicholas: A Closer Look at Christmas

Joe Wheeler & Jim Rosenthal
published by Thomas Nelson, Nashville
Everyone loves the character known variously as Santa Claus, Father Christmas, and Jolly Old St. Nicholas. He brings presents to children and joy to people all over the world. But he is a mysterious figure, a children's myth that often seems to detract from the religious meaning of Christmas. This book changes that perception by recovering the historical St. Nicholas and providing a closer look at Christmas traditions with colorful photographs, illustrations, and stories. This coffee table-sized book makes a delightful gift.

The Best Christmas Pageant Ever

Barbara Robinson
Published by Avon Books
The Herdman family children were the black sheep of the community. What a shock when they took part in the Christmas pageant! They didn't even know what a shepherd was, much less about the true story of Christmas. Somehow, amidst the chaotic rehearsals, the pageant turned out better than ever! The baby Jesus was burped instead of cuddled and they thought a ham was a much better present than perfumed oil, but Imogene Herdman's tears literally made the pageant a beacon of Christ's light.

The Case for Christmas

Lee Strobel
Published by Zondervan, Grand Rapids, 1998
In the same style as A Case for Christ and A Case for Faith, Lee Stobel examines the evidence for the authenticity of Christ. In this small book, suitable for gift-giving, Stobel makes a case for Christ's incarnation based on eyewitness evidence, scientific evidence, profile evidence and fingerprint evidence (Did Jesus uniquely match the identity of the Messiah?) The Case for Christmas invites the reader to consider why Christmas matters in the first place.

The Guideposts Christmas Treasury

Guideposts Associates, Inc.
Out of print but available used through Amazon.
A compilation of delightful Christmas stories to be read and reread.

Two from Galilee

Marjorie Holmes
Fleming H. Revell, Old Tappan, 1972
This classic is a heartwarming weaving of fact and fiction told as only Marjorie Holmes can.
It is a book to be read year after year. Joseph and Mary become real people who suffer the humiliation of Mary's "untimely" pregnancy.

DVD's

Christmas with a Capital "C"

Christmas has always been a time of love and tradition in small town Trapper Falls, hometown of Mayor Dan Reed. With his brother

Greg, they drape the town in Christmas cheer concentrating on the Nativity scene. When Dan's high school rival Mitch Bright returns home after 20 years, he takes offense to seeing the town's Nativity scene in violation of separation of church and state. Mitch wants the Nativity scene removed and the word Christmas switched to Happy Holidays. Dan's wife Kristen and their daughter show the true meaning of Christmas by launching a "Christmas with a Capital "C" campaign as an effort to keep the town together. Trapper Falls learns the lesson that with the arrival of Christmas, good will was to be given to all, even those whose hearts seem closed to Him.

The Grinch who Stole Christmas

Every Who down in Whoville liked Christmas a lot. This joyous, heart-tickling holiday event based on Dr. Seuss' beloved book and featuring the voice of Boris Karloff has delighted viewers of all ages since its 1966 debut. The fun begins when the grumpy, grouchy, Yule-hating Grinch plots to ruin the Whos' Christmas. Can he steal their holiday spirit by stealing their holiday treats and gifts? Or does Christmas... perhaps...mean a little bit more?

The Nativity Story

Powerful, timeless and visually magnificent, The Nativity Story is a beautiful telling of one of the world's most familiar stories. Epic in scope, yet intimate in its portrayal of the historical, holy family, this wonderful DVD is a family feature that will be cherished for years to come.

The Star of Bethlehem

Frederick A. Larson has done extensive research to unlock the mystery of the world's most famous star. The history and Biblical connection of the star of Bethlehem is sure to amaze all who view this DVD. Appropriate for older children and adults.

NOTES

Chapter 1 A Look over Our Collective Shoulders

1. Ken Potts, Detroit Daily Herald, Dec. 1992.

Chapter 3 Traditions to Treasure

1. *A Family Advent, Keeping the Savior in the Season*, (Nashville, TN: Thomas Nelson Publishers, 2008), pp. 18.
2. Daily Word, A Unity Publication, May 3, 2013, p.14.

Chapter 5 The Stress Mess, Cleaning it Up

1. Doc Childre, founder Institute of Heartmath, Detroit Free Press, Dec., 1998.
   (See also Doc Childre's book *Freeze Frame, One Minute Stress Management*).
   Lambreth Hochwalk, Prevention Magazine, May 2013, p. 136.
   Michael Card, God's Vitamin "C" for the Christmas Spirit, (Lancaster, PA: Starburst Publishers, 1996), pp. 135-136.
2. *The Compassionate Friends* Newsletter, 1996 Holiday Issue. To order the newsletter, call the National Office at 630-990-0010 or www.compassionatefriends.org.
3. David Jeremiah, Turning Points Magazine and Devotional, Dec., 2012, pp 23-24.

4. Jerry Gjesvold helps companies across Oregon create and manage their drug-free workplace policies and programs. More information is available at Serenity Lane website at www.serenitylane.org.

Chapter 6 A Guide to Managing Holiday Grief

1. *Blue Christmas Celebration*, a Hospice of Holland publication.
2. Jerry Gjesvold, *Making it through the Toughest Days of Grief.* This book can be ordered through Centering Corp at 866-218-0101 or www.centering.org.

Chapter 7 What to Say, What to Do?

1. Joe Wheeler and Jim Rosenthal, *St. Nicholas, A Closer Look at Christmas,* Nelson Reference & Electronic, a division of Thomas Nelson Publishers, 2005), pp.XI-XV.
2. A Dutch Christmas, The Legend of Sinterklaas, Julie Nelis Steggerda, p. 1.
3. Ibid., pp.6-7.
   See the website: www.dutchvillage.com to learn more about this delightful Dutch amusement village with gift shops and restaurant located on U.S. 31 and James St. in Holland, Michigan.
4. Two excellent resources for young children in describing the relationship between the two gift-giving icons is, *Santa, Are you for Real?*, Harold Mira and *St. Nicholas: A Closer Look at Christmas,* Joe Wheeler and Jim Rosenthal. The latter is a coffee table book to be read and reread. Discover more information about St. Nicholas by visiting the websites devoted to him at www.stnicholascenter.org. and www.stnicholassociety.com
5. Sue Halpern, *Good Housekeeping, Dec. 1998, The December Dilemma.*

Chapter 8 Gift Giving Revisited

1. Henri J. M. Nouwen, excerpt from the article,"The Spirituality of Waiting" in *Weavings,* January 1987, The Upper Room, Nashville, Tennessee, 1987.

Chapter 9 Christmas Trivia

1. Melissa Wilson, *God's Vitamin "C" for the Christmas Spirit,* (Lancaster, PA: Starburst Publishers, 1996), pp. 118.
2. Ibid., pp. 90-91.
3. Ibid., pp. 19.
4. Ibid., p. 23.
5. David Jeremiah, *Turning Points Magazine and Devotional,* December 2011, p. 10.

Chapter 10 Celebrate Epiphany

1. Dana Reynolds, *Be an Angel,* (New York, Simon & Schuster, 1994), p. 91.